How to improve your soccer team players

By Raed Thaher

ELITE BOOK FOR ELITE PLAYERS

MORE Than 60 Different Sessions For Soccer Players Need

ISBN: 978-1-365-91681-6

Table of Contents

Introduction

A soccer player needs to master many different skills in order to be successful on the soccer field. Once a player learns a skill he will also need to maintain it.

The best way for doing that is to participate in various drills. The fundamental thing a soccer player need to know about soccer drills is that he really needs to work hard during them in order to develop his skills.

I know by experience that many soccer players do not actually focus on the drills. Instead, they see them as something that needs to be done during the practice and then forgets about them. The danger with this behavior is that the players will become less focused during the real games which will impact negatively on their performance.

You see, it is not enough to practice on various drills if you never reflect over how you can use them in real game situations. Every time you participate in a drill, you need to imagine how this drill could help you during the games.

To state an example let's discuss how a simple shooting drill can make you think outside the box. During a shooting drill, you will, (in most cases), kick the ball with maximum possible power because you probably think that the harder the shot is the bigger the chance for scoring a goal.

However, you should be aware of that getting that ball on the goal is much more important than kicking the ball with tremendous power. So, by actually reflecting over the drill, you have discovered that a hard shot is not a guarantee for scoring more goals

If you start to reflect over the drills you will soon notice that you are actually using what you've learned during the drills in real soccer games. So, don't just perform the drills, be sure to know the benefits of them.

Passing The Ball

In the early days of modern soccer the game was all about dribbling and tackling. Then the Scottish invented the passing game and became pretty much unbeatable. Soon everyone else followed suit. The ability to move the ball up the field at speed from player to player has remained a key part of the game ever since. Quite simply, if a team can't pass accurately, they are not going to win...

Passing can be done with any part of the foot. The instep is generally used for a long ball, the inside of the foot for a sager, shorter pass. The outside of the show is often an effective method of curving a pass and surprising the opposition – a well placed back-heel kick can completely deceive a defense. You can even pass with other parts of your body – your head is a vital tool, as is your chest.

Passing also enables a team to keep possession and it is worth emphasizing that a team cannot score if it does not have possession. A well-placed pass from midfield to a point in front of an attacker's run can set up a goal, and the ability to do passes like this is one of the most prized assets in the game. One much-maligned but very useful method of passing is the ling ball. This can vary from an aimless "thump" up front by a beleaguered defender to an inch-perfect diagonal ball from a gifted midfielder.

Like any other aspect of the game, passing in all its various forms must be practiced before any player can be sure of being effective in a game.

Passing training sessions

Ground passing

Ground Passes

Key Factors :

TIME 30mins

1. The kicking foot ankle firm and at right angles to the ball.
2. The non-kicking foot placed along side of the ball.
3. Strike the ball at the mid line.
4. Head steady with the eyes on the ball.

Equipment : Grids created from cones, 10 balls

Practice Sequence 1: 10 minutes 2 players pass to each other using first right then left foot.	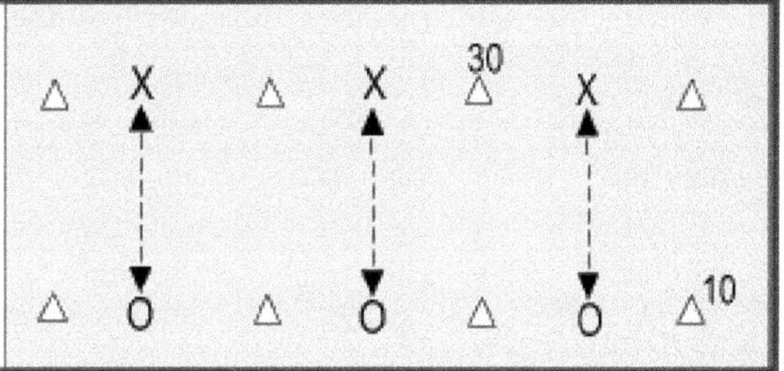
Practice Sequence 2: 10 minutes X passes the ball to O. X moves to the other side of the grid to receive the returned pass from O. X controls the ball and returns the pass to O and continues to run between the grid.	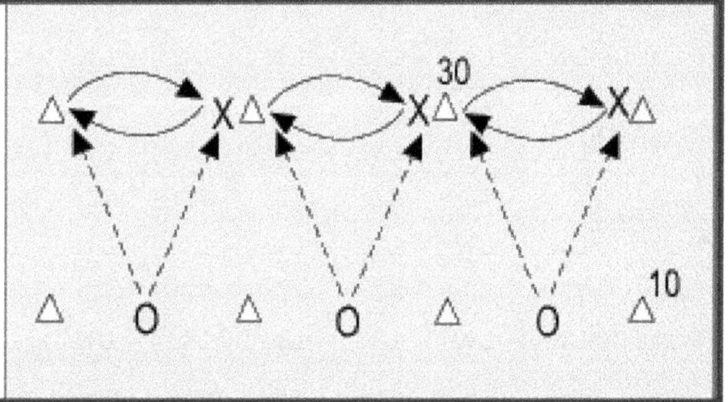
Practice Sequence 3: 10 minutes O makes a diagonal pass to X. X runs across the grid to receive the ball. O runs to the other side of the grid to receive a square pass from X.	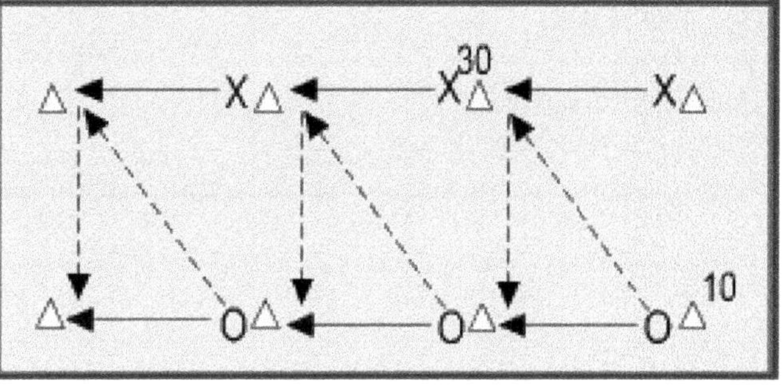

Lofted Passes

Key Factors : TIME 30mins

1. The kicking foot should strike through the bottom half of the ball.
2. The non-kicking foot placed slightly behind the ball.
3. The body should lean slightly back.
4. Head steady with the eyes on the ball.

Equipment : Grids created from cones, 10 balls

Practice Sequence 1: 10 minutes 2 players pass to each other using lofted passes both trapping and returning the pass. Both players should use all three techniques as described.	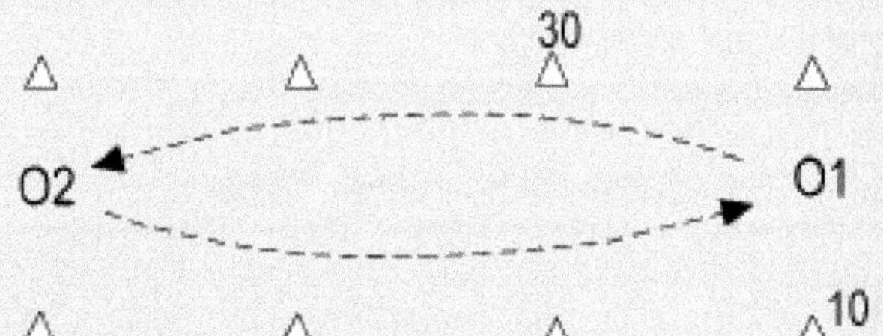
Practice Sequence 2: 10 minutes X passes the ball to O1 and the O players make lofted passes to each other, while X moves inside the middle grid threatening the passes. Both players should use all three techniques as described.	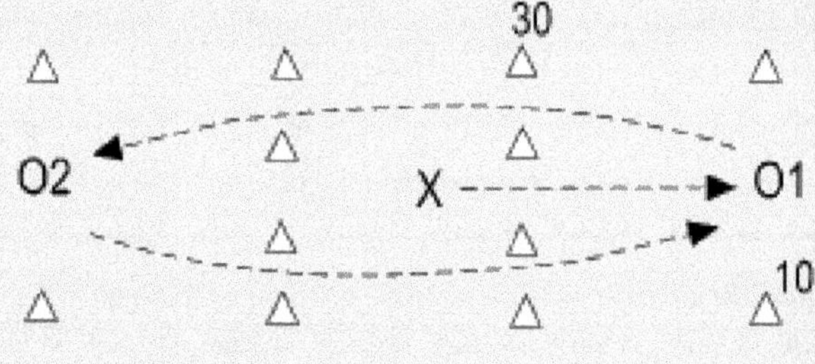
Practice Sequence 3: 10 minutes X1 passes the ball to O1 and the O players make lofted passes to each other, while the X players move inside the middle grid threatening the passes. Both of the O players should use all three techniques as described.	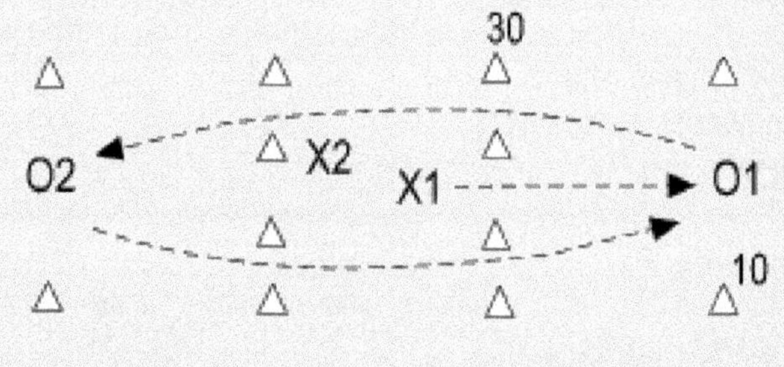

One touch practice

One Touch Practice

TIME 30mins

Key Factors :

1. Eyes on the ball while kicking.
2. Body over the ball.
3. Non kicking foot square on the ball.
4. Pace and accuracy.

Equipment : Grids created from cones, 10 balls ,bibs

Practice Sequence 1: 10 minutes X passes to O using just one touch of the ball. The ball is then passed between the players using just one touch with pace and accuracy.	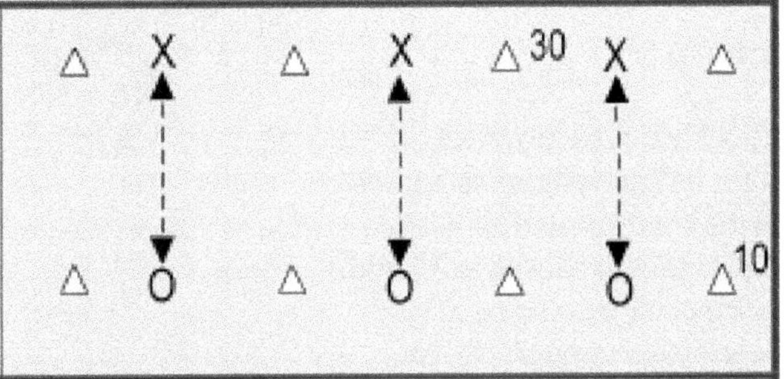
Practice Sequence 2: 10 minutes X1 passes to X2 who passes to X3. X3 passes the ball back to X1 who passes to X4. X4 passes to X3 who passes to X1. Then continue in this sequence.	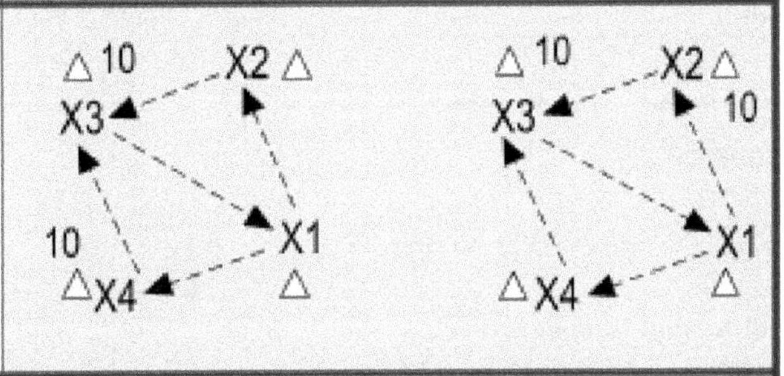
Practice Sequence 3: 10 minutes X and O run alone the side of the cones passing the ball to each other between the cones but only using one touch of the ball.	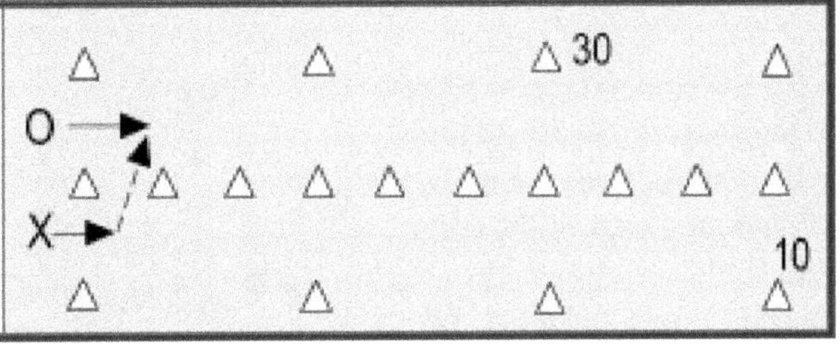

Passing and Running

Key Factors : TIME 30mins

1. A ground pass with accuracy and good pace.
2. Trap the ball with one touch and pass the ball with the second touch.
3. Keep body over the ball with eyes on the ball.
4. Run at controlled speed in opposite direction to the ball.

Equipment : Grids created from cones, 10 balls ,bibs

Practice Sequence 1:
15 minutes
X1 passes to X2 and runs to join X4.
X2 receives the ball and passes to X3 and runs back to the cone vacated by X1.
X3 receives the ball and passes to X4 and runs back to the cone vacated by X2.
Continue the exercise using all players around the grid

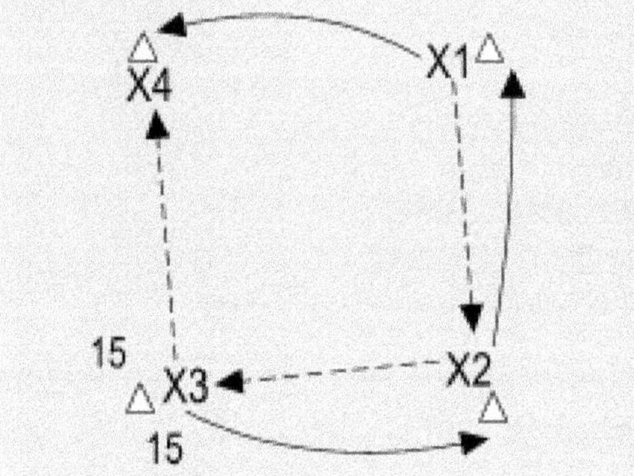

Practice Sequence 2:
15 minutes
Start the sequence with X1 and X5 and play with 2 balls.
X1 passes to X2 and runs to join X8.
At the same time X5 passes to X6 and runs to join X4.
X2 receives the ball and passes to X3 and runs back to the cone vacated by X1.
At the same time X6 receives the ball and passes to X7 and runs back to the cone vacated by X5.
Keep the play continuous but if the play gets out of sequence or the balls go out of the grid start again.

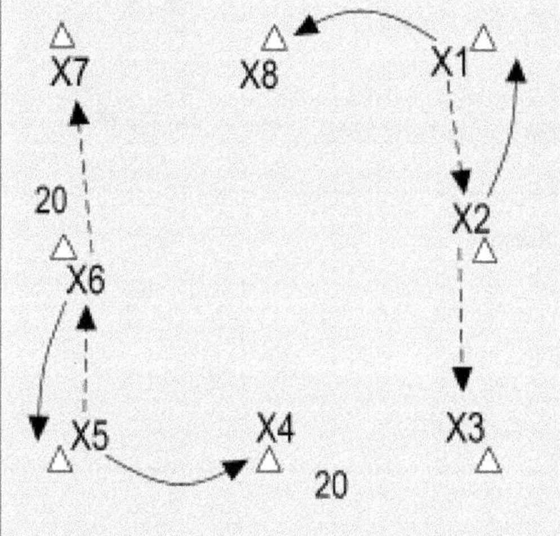

Groung Passing Accuracy

Ground Passing Accuracy

Key Factors : TIME 30mins

1. Ground passes with accuracy and pace.
2. When passing keep the eyes on the ball with the body up and over the ball.
3. Run at controlled speed to the next point to receive the ball.
4. Be relaxed and confident to pass and receive the ball.

Equipment : Goal and penalty area , 10 balls , cones, bibs

Practice Sequence 1:
15 minutes
The server plays the ball to X1 who controls the ball and runs to make a pass through the cones to X2.
X2 runs along side the cones to receive the ball half way along the grid area.
X1 continues running to receive the return pass from X2 and a makes a shot on the goal.
Alternate the start right and left.

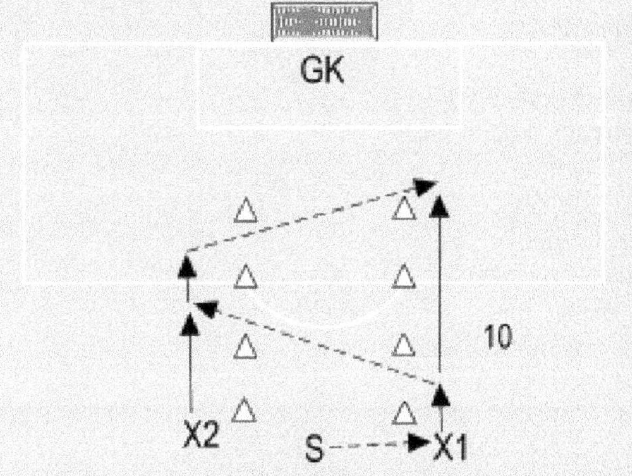

Practice Sequence 2:
15 minutes
The server plays the ball to X1 who controls the ball and runs to make a pass through the cones to X2.
X2 starts at the opposite side of the grid and runs towards X1 to receive the ball.
X1 continues running to receive the return pass from X2 and a makes a shot on the goal.
Alternate the start right and left.

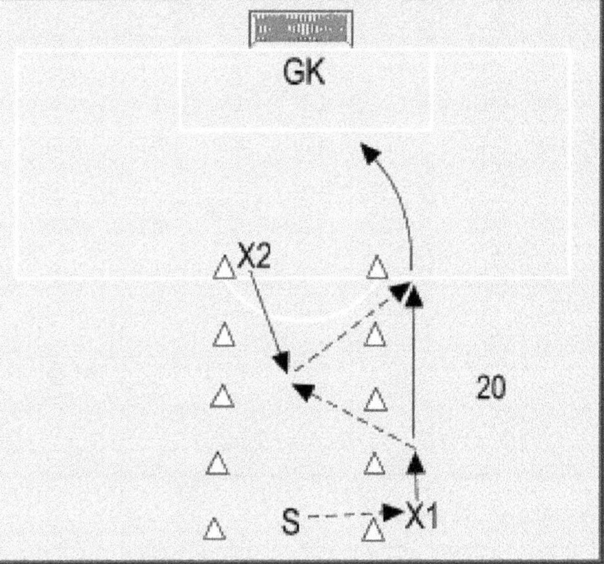

Lofted Forward Passing

Key Factors TIME 30mins:

1. Head up to view the field of play.
2. Play a forward lofted pass.
3. Timing and accuracy of the pass.
4. Play to the receiving player or in front, for the player to run on to.

Equipment : Goal and penalty area , 10 balls , cones, bibs

Practice Sequence 1:
10 minutes
The players take turns making a lofted pass into the opposing square.
The players make lofted passes to each other concentrating on the lofted passing technique.
Encourage players to alternate using both left and right foot.

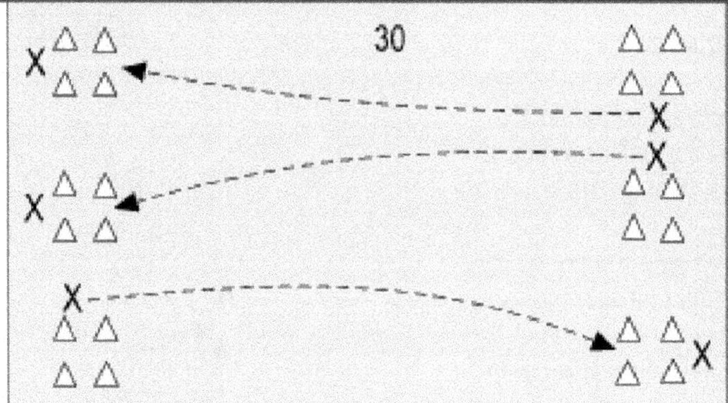

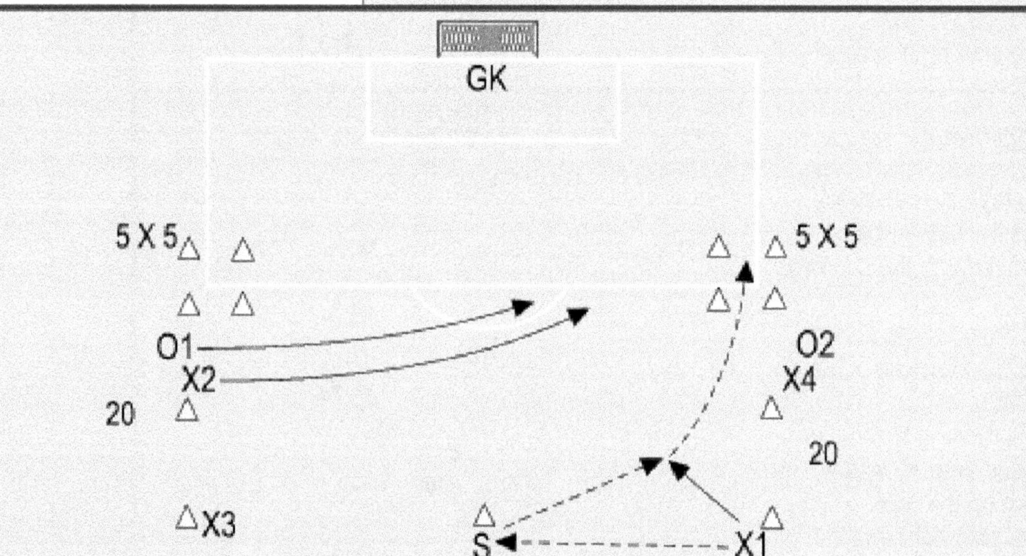

Practice Sequence 2: 20 minutes
X1 passes the ball to sever and runs to receive the returned pass.
X2 runs across the field to receive a lofted pass in the far corner of the penalty area.
The O players should defend to prevent a shot on goal.
Alternate the start both left and right.

Passing As A Group

Passing as a Group

Key Factors :

TIME 30mins

1. Passes should be accurate and with good pace.
2. First touch on the ball.
3. Control the ball in the direction of the run.
4. Create space off the ball to receive a pass.

Equipment : Grids created from cones, 10 balls ,bibs

Practice Sequence 1:
10 minutes
The X players should pass the ball to the opposite X player and then run to the end of the other line.
Count the number of passes before the ball is lost, for competition.

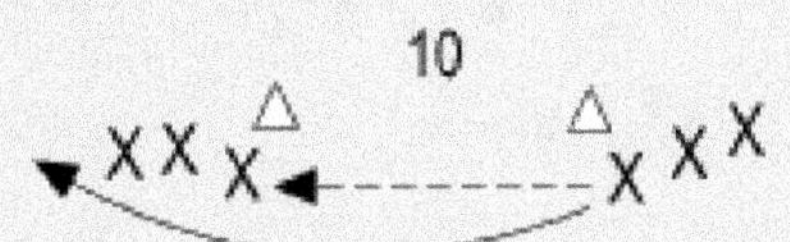

Practice Sequence 2:
10 minutes
The X players should try to make 10 consecutive passes to each other across the grid then rotate the defender.
If the defender intercepts the ball then the defender is rotated automatically.
The X players are only allowed to run between the cones.

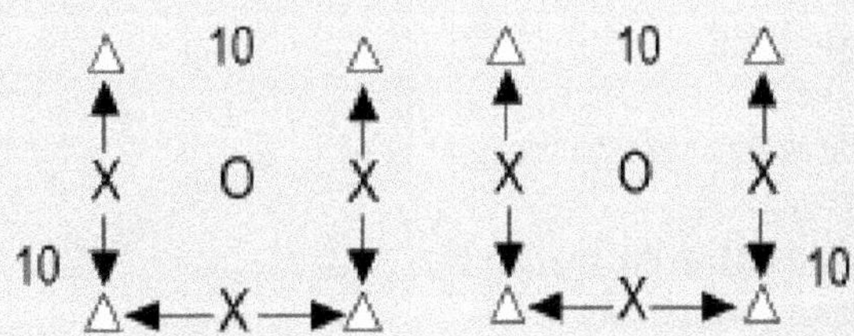

Practice Sequence 3:
10 minutes
4 v 4 inside a 20 X 20 yard grid with four goals.
The X players should attack the 2 goals to right and the O players should attack the 2 goals to the left.

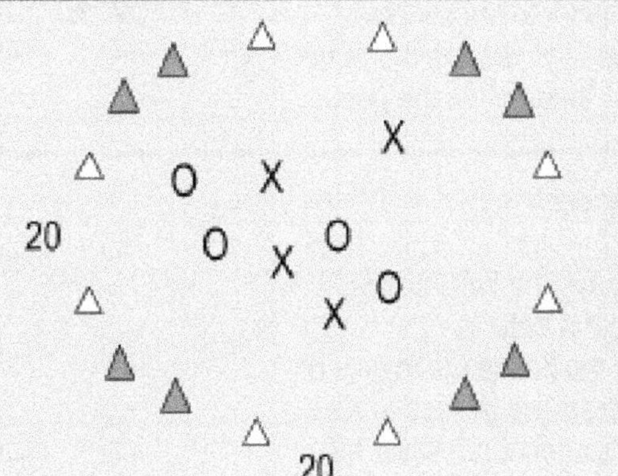

Running at Angles

Key Factors : TIME 30mins

1. Timing and accuracy of the passes and the pace on the ball.
2. Timing and angle of the runs.
3. Run quickly but at a controlled speed.
4. Create space away from the opponent to receive and pass the ball.

Equipment : Goal and penalty area , 10 balls , cones, bibs

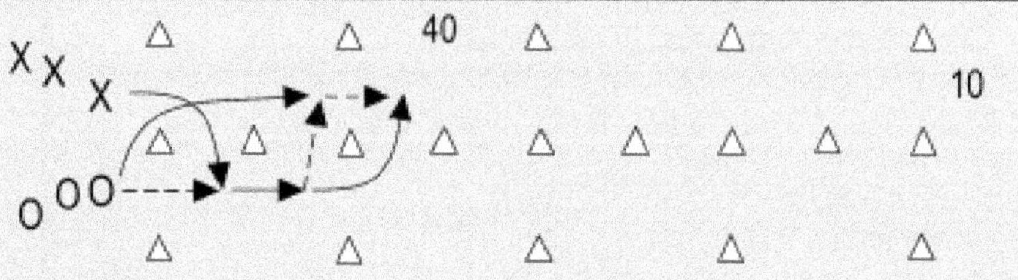

Practice Sequence 1: 10 minutes
O passes the ball directly along the line of the cones for X to run through the cones onto the ball. O then runs around to the opposite side of the cones to receive a return pass through the cones. O plays the ball along the line of cones and X plays the ball through the cones.

Practice Sequence 2:
10 minutes
The server plays the ball into the path of X1 to run onto.
X1 runs with the ball to the middle of the penalty area and passes to X2.
X1 makes a diagonal run while X2 who controls the ball and passes it into the path of X1.
X2 makes a run into the middle of the penalty area to receive the return pass from X1 to shoot on the goal.

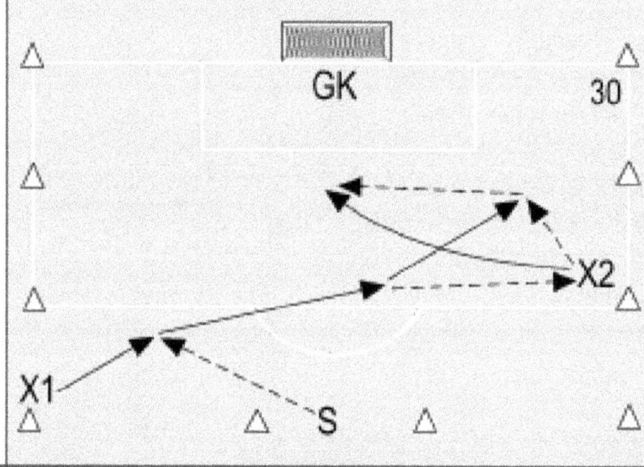

Practice Sequence 3:
10 minutes
The server plays the ball into the path of X1 to run onto.
X1 runs with the ball to the middle of the penalty area and passes to X2.
X1 makes a diagonal run while X2 controls the ball and passes it into the path of X1.
X2 makes a run into the middle of the penalty area to receive the return pass from X1 to shoot on the goal.
O1 and O2 must prevent the X players from scoring a goal.

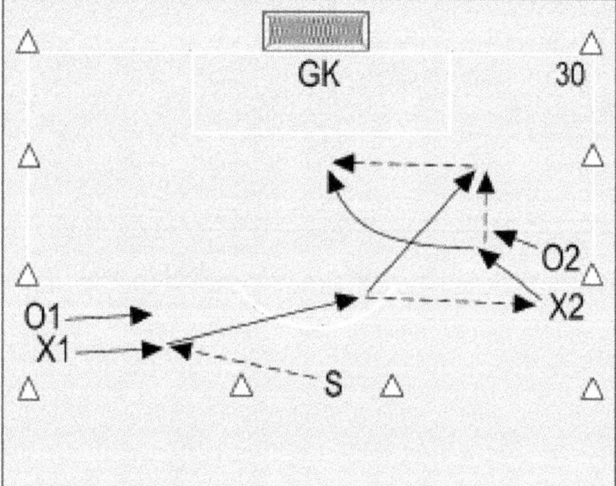

Forward passing

Key Factors :

TIME 20mins

1. Control the ball with the first touch using the outside foot.
2. Keep an open body stance and view the playing situation.
3. Select passing option.
4. All players create space to receive the ball from a forward pass.

Equipment : Small sided field 60 X 40 created with cones, divided into thirds, 10 balls, bibs

Starting Position :
For left side practice, X2 passes to O6 who passes to the goalkeeper and the goalkeeper throws the ball to X1.
For right side practice, X1 passes to O5 who passes to the goalkeeper and the goalkeeper throws the ball to X2

Practice Sequence :
The goalkeeper should only throw the ball to either X1 or X2.
X1 or X2 should create space to receive the ball while other players create space to receive the forward pass.

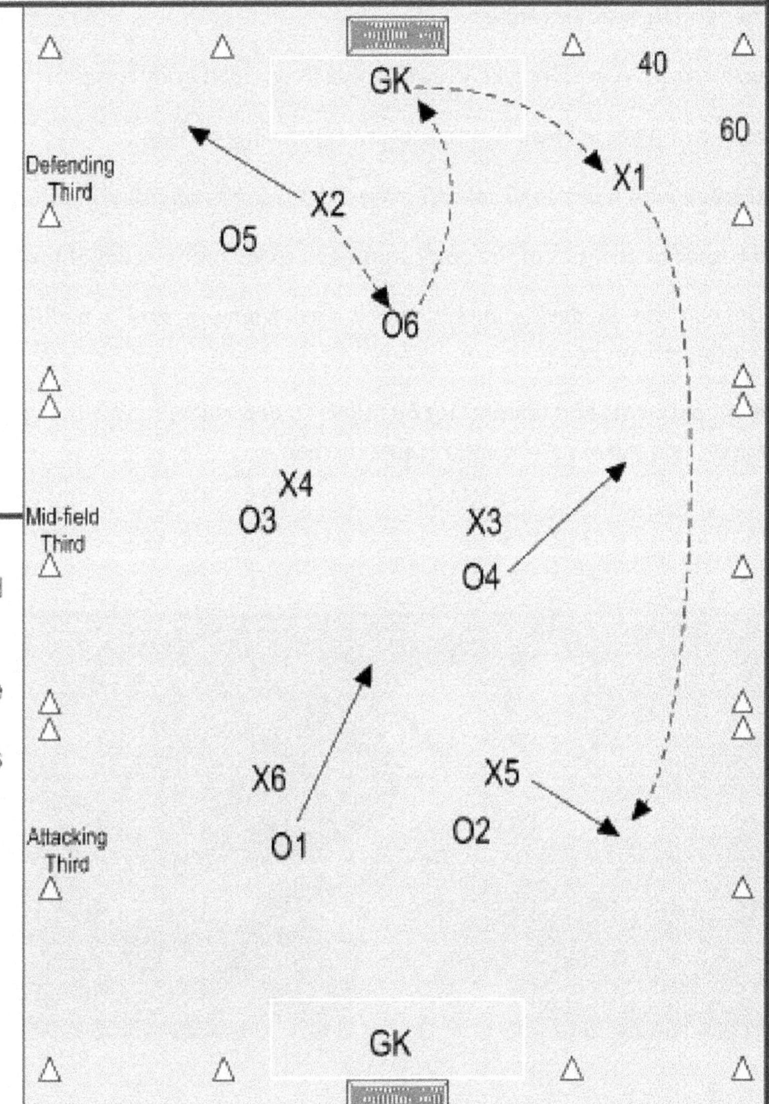

Player Ball Control

In today's game of soccer spaces become tighter and the pace is higher. Getting and keeping the ball under control is an important skill a football player has to learn and in response to this, an essential skill a coach should teach players of all positions is to develop the ability to handle the ball with a constructive first touch to promptly decide on the following move (dribble, pass or shoot) without giving the opponent the chance to gain possession. The drills in this section will increase your players' comfort level on the ball working with various parts including the feet, thigh, chest and head which are all relevant to skills the players will need on the field

Key Coaching Points for Ball Control:

1 - stay on toes and be ready to adjust

2 - move towards the ball to control early and to be in an open body position

3 - move into line of flight of the ball and present controlling surface

4 - eyes on the ball with head up to select next option (use peripheral vision)

5 - relax and withdraw the part of the body contacted to kill momentum of the ball

6 - cushion the ball into the desired direction and away from pressure (a bad first touch might result in losing possession)

7 - be aware of opponents and teammates positions to determine next move (pass, shoot or dribble) know your next move before you receive the ball.

Trapping The Ball

Trapping the Ball

TIME 40mins

Key Factors :

1. Keep the body square to the ball.
2. Cushion the impact of the ball.
3. Use the specific part of the body to trap the ball.
4. Head steady with eyes on the ball.

Equipment : Grids created from cones, 10 balls

Practice Sequence 1: 10 minutes O throws the ball to X who traps the ball with the foot and passes the ball back	△ 10 △ O ------► X △ △10
Practice Sequence 2: 10 minutes O throws the ball to X who traps the ball with the knee and passes the ball back.	△ 10 △ O ------► X △ △10
Practice Sequence 3: 10 minutes O throws the ball to X who traps the ball with the chest and passes the ball back.	△ 10 △ O ------► X △ 10 △10
Practice Sequence 4: 10 minutes O throws the ball to X who traps the ball with the chest then drops the ball to the knee and ends up with a trap of the ball at the feet. X should end up passing the ball back.	△ △ O ------► X △ △10

Dribbling

Key Factors : TIME 30mins

1. Close control of the ball.
2. Run straight at the opponent.
3. Slow in fast out.
4. Fake out opponent.

Equipment : Grids created from cones, 10 balls ,bibs

Practice Sequence 1: 10 minutes 5 Players dribble the ball inside the grid turning first with the inside of the foot then with the outside of the foot. Each player must keep control of the ball without touching other players.	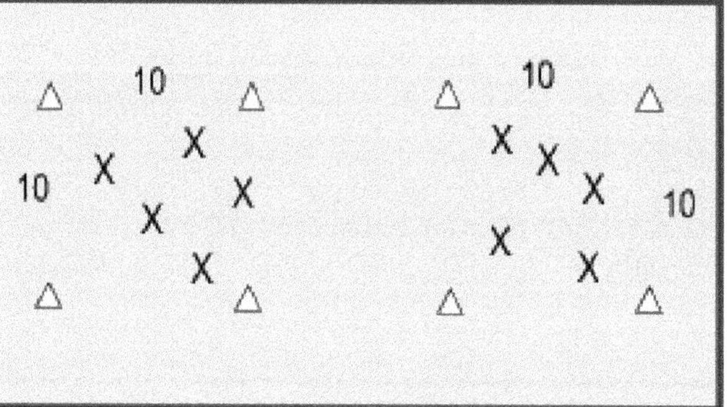 10 10 10 10 X X X X X X X X X X X X
Practice Sequence 2: 10 minutes Server S passes the ball to X who attempts to dribble past O to the small goal at the other end.	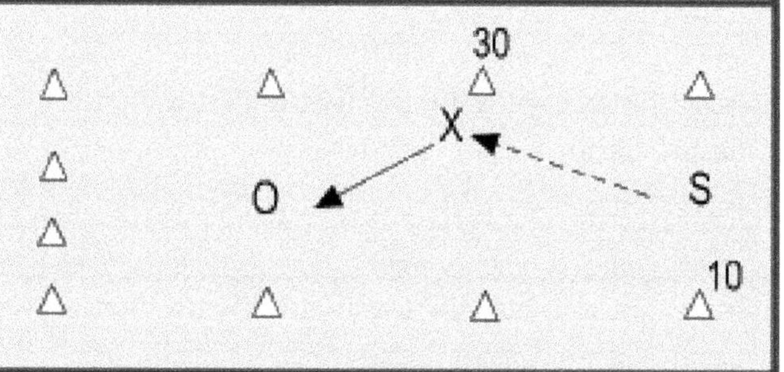 30 X O S 10
Practice Sequence 3: 10 minutes Server X2 passes the ball to X1 who attempts to dribble past O1 and O2 to the small goal at the other end. Both X1 and X2 play against O1 and O2.	30 X1 O1 X2 O2 10

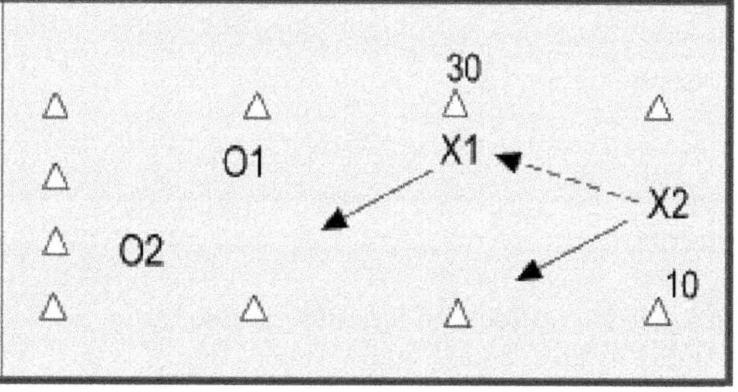

Dribbling Techniques

Key Factors : TIME 30mins

1. Approach the opponent at controlled speed.
2. Unbalance the opponent just out of tackling distance using one technique.
3. While opponent is unbalanced change direction.
4. Explode into the space behind the opponent.

Equipment : Grids created from cones, 10 balls

Practice Sequence 1: 10 minutes The X player dribbles using the Matthews move against the defender O. Techniques of the Mathews Move: Move the ball with the inside of the foot and drop the opposite shoulder and then change direction and kick the ball with outside of the same foot and move in the same direction.	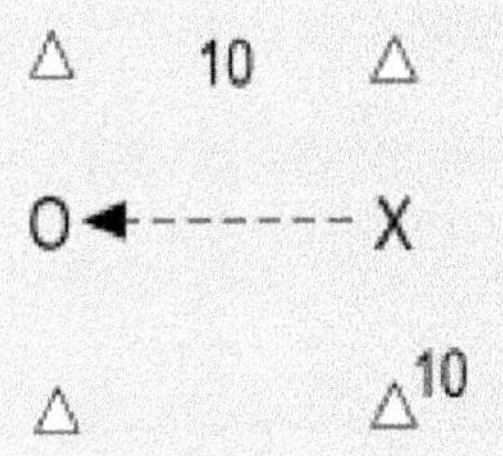 △ 10 △ O◄------X △ △10
Practice Sequence 2: 10 minutes The X player dribbles using the Scissors move against the defender O. Techniques of the Scissors Move : Play the ball in front and pretend to play the ball with the outside of the foot but instead step over the ball and play the ball with outside of the opposite foot and move in the same direction.	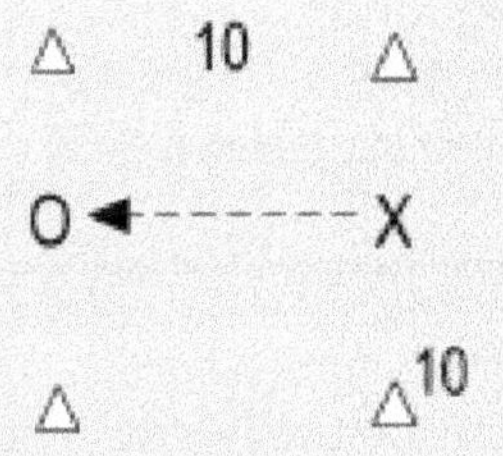 △ 10 △ O◄------X △ △10
Practice Sequence 3: 10 minutes The X player dribbles using the Gruyff Move against the defender O. Techniques of the Gruyff Move : Run with the ball directly at the opponent and pretend to shoot but with the same foot drag the ball back behind the opposite leg. Turn in the opposite direction and move away with the ball using the opposite foot.	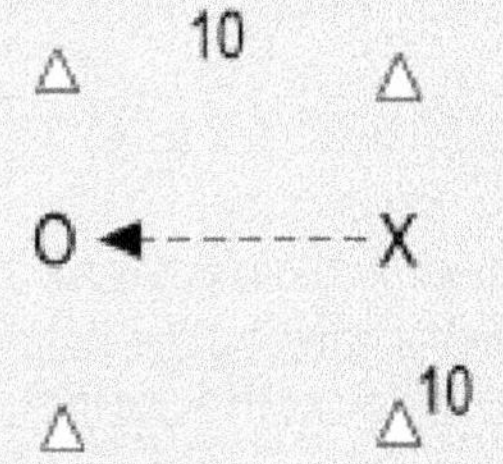 △ 10 △ O◄------X △ △10

Throw-ins

Key Factors : TIME 30mins

1. Throw the ball from behind the head with both hands on the ball.
2. Keep both feet in contact with the ground perhaps dragging one foot
3. The ball should be thrown to the receiving player at most direct angle
4. Throw the ball hard enough for the receiving player to control the ball.

Equipment : Grids created from cones, 10 balls, bibs

Practice Sequence 1:
10 minutes
2 players throw-in the ball to each other concentrating on correct throwing action.

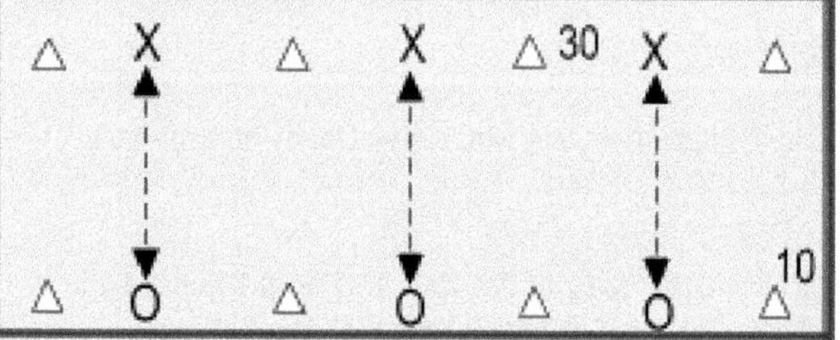

Practice Sequence 2:
10 minutes
The player O throws the ball to the oncoming player X.
The X player starts at a distance of 20 yards and then increases it to 30 yards.

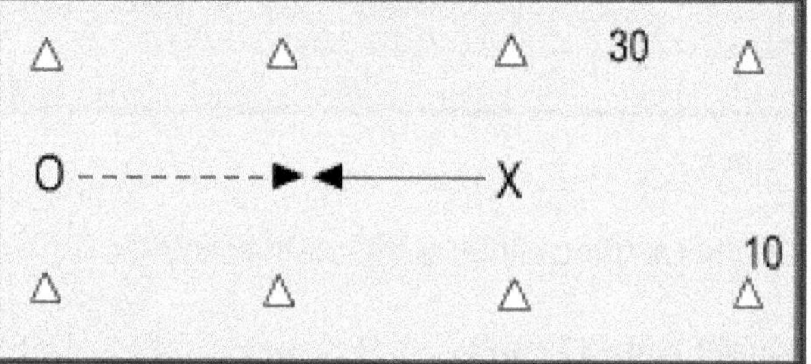

Practice Sequence 3:
10 minutes
X1 throws to the ball to the oncoming player X2.
X2 starts at 20 yards distance while the defender O starts from a distance of 30 yards.
X2 should play the ball back to X1 the thrower and start again.
The O defender should pressure X2 to prevent X2 from receiving the ball.

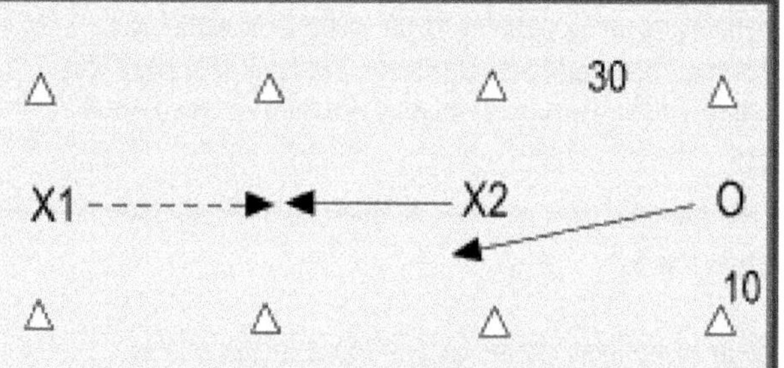

Ball Control while Running

TIME 30mins

Key Factors :

1. Body square to the ball.
2. Run at controlled speed.
3. Bring ball under control first time.
4. Head steady with eyes on the ball.

Equipment : Grids created from cones, 10 balls

Practice Sequence 1:
10 minutes
X runs between the 2 servers S who are making ground passes, and makes a foot trap with the ball, returns the ball with a ground pass to the server

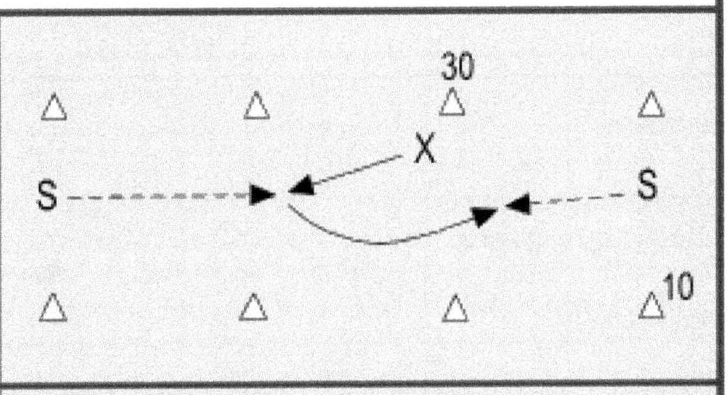

Practice Sequence 2:
10 minutes
X runs between the 2 servers S who are making throw-ins, and makes a chest trap with the ball and returns the ball with a ground pass to the server.

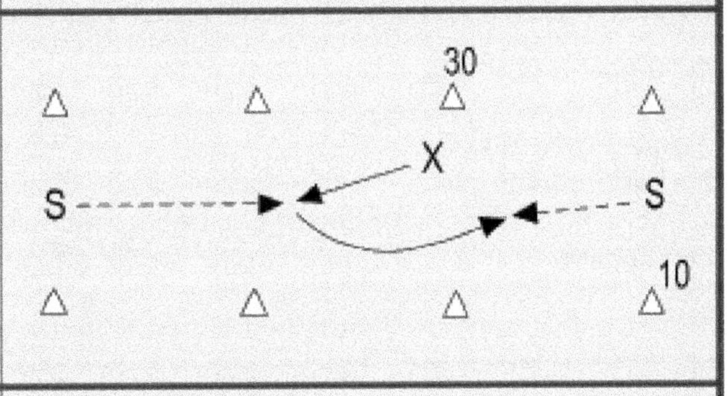

Practice Sequence 3:
10 minutes
X runs between the 2 servers S who are making throw-ins, heads the ball back to the server.

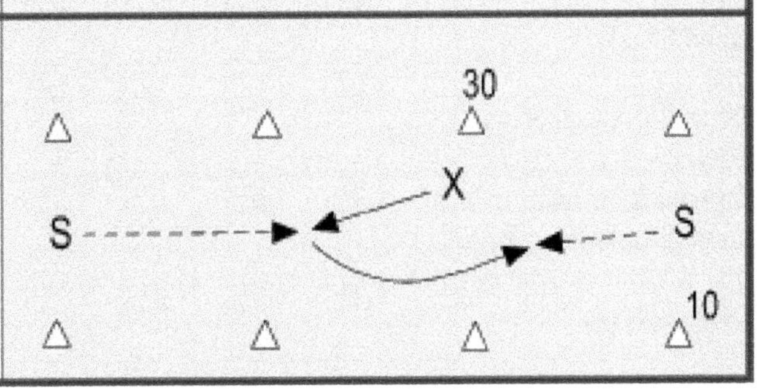

Heading the Ball

TIME 30mins

Key Factors :

1. Attack the ball.
2. Head the ball with the upper part of the forehead.
3. Body square to the ball.
4. Keep eyes on the ball.

Equipment : Grids created from cones, 10 balls, bibs

Practice Sequence 1: 10 minutes The server makes a throw-in to O who heads the ball up and out of the area. Switch between servers.	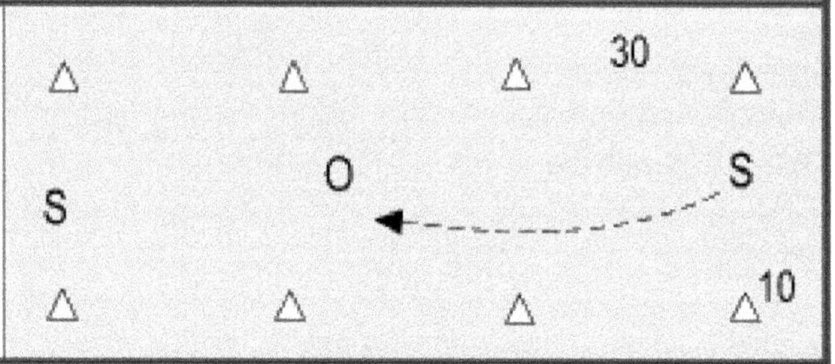 30 O S S 10
Practice Sequence 2: 10 minutes The server makes a throw-in to X who heads the ball down into the goal. Switch between servers.	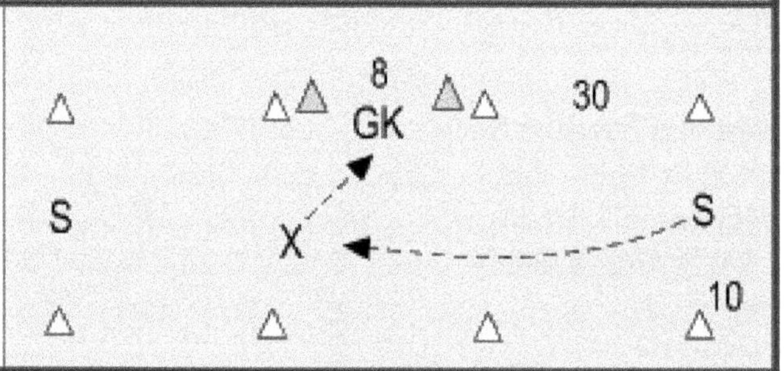 8 GK 30 S S X 10
Practice Sequence 3: 10 minutes The defender or the attacker must make a header. The server makes a throw-in to X and O and both should try to head the ball. Switch between servers.	8 GK 30 O S S X 10

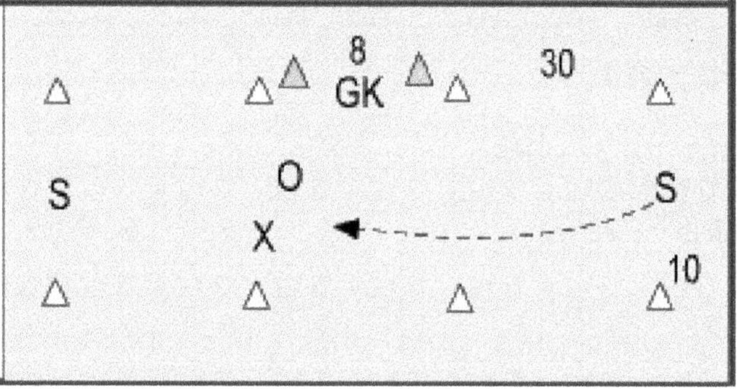

Individual Running With Ball Handling

Individual Running with Ball Handling

Key Factors :

TIME 30mins

1. Close control of the ball.
2. Eyes on the ball while controlling or kicking the ball.
3. Good body balance.
4. Run at controlled speed.

Equipment : Grids created from cones, 10 balls

Practice Sequence 1:
10 minutes
Each player takes turns in running while alternately kicking the ball first with the right then the left foot.

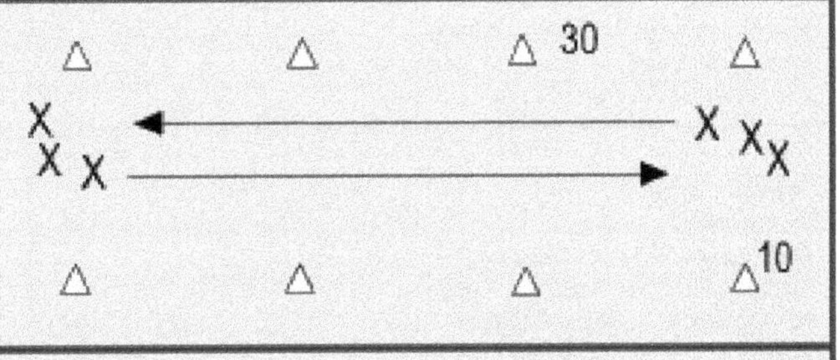

Practice Sequence 2:
10 minutes
Each player take turns in running backwards while alternately dragging the ball with top of the foot first with the right then the left foot.

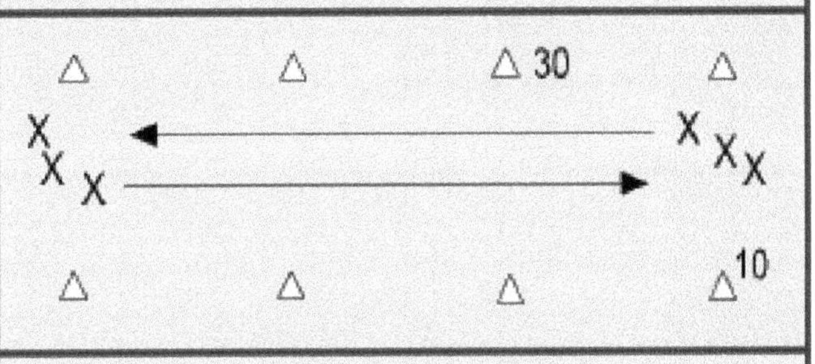

Practice Sequence 3:
10 minutes
Each player take turns in running between the cones, kicking the ball between the cones, using the inside of the foot furthest away from the cones.

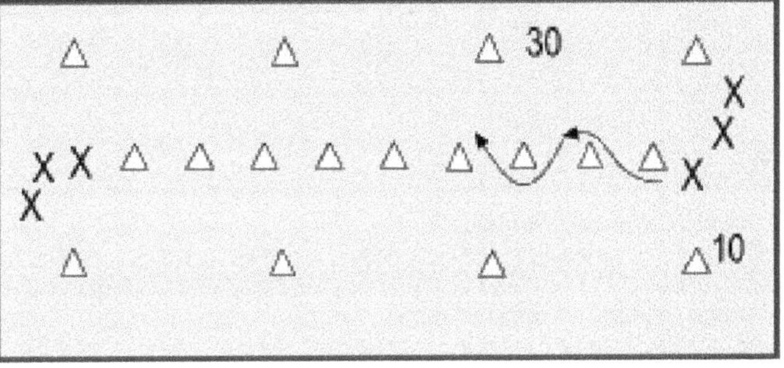

Running with the Ball

Key Factors : TIME 30mins

1. Kick the ball into space in front with the outside of the foot.
2. Run quickly but at controlled speed.
3. Avoid opponents by running into space.
4. Keep head up while not kicking the ball to view the field.

Equipment : Grids created from cones, 10 balls ,bibs

Practice Sequence 1:
10 minutes
One player at a time collects the ball and runs through the gates at controlled speed.
The ball is played to the next player and the first player joins the team.

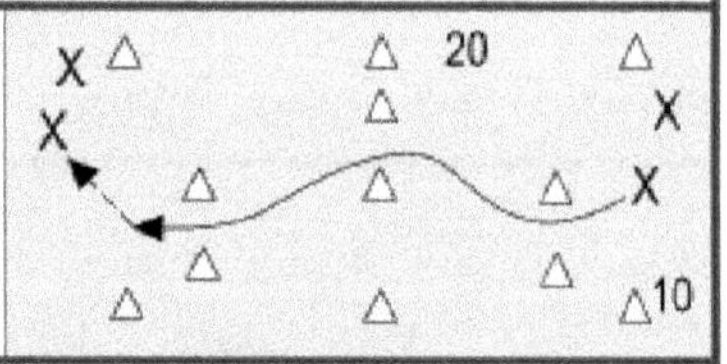

Practice Sequence 2:
10 minutes
One player from each of the three teams take turns in crossing the grid running with the ball avoiding other players without losing the ball.
When the player reaches the other side of the grid the ball is passed to the next player.

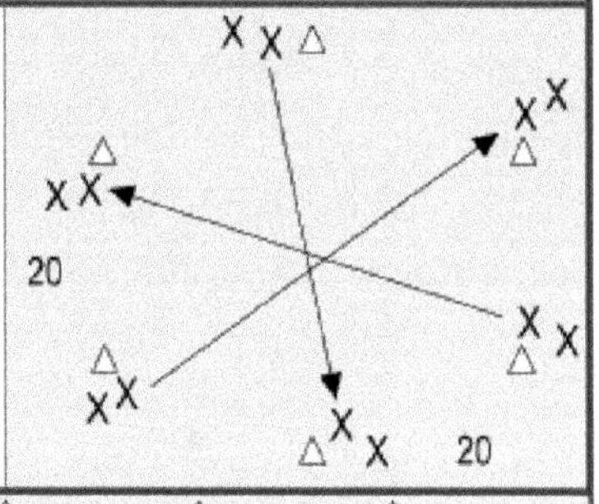

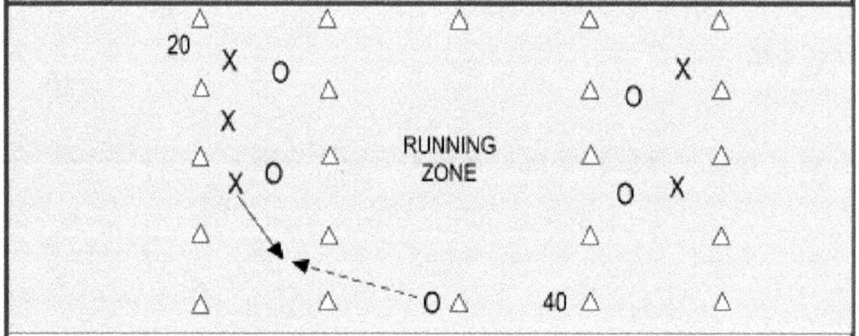

Practice Sequence 3: 10 minutes
The object of the practice is for the X players in one end grid to play against the O players and release one of their team to run with the ball through the running zone and join the other X players in the other end grid.
To start the O player in the running zone passes the ball to an X player in the end grid with the most X players, and the X team should play against the O players to release one of them from the grid to run with the ball through the running zone. The O defenders must stay inside their respective grids but prevent the X players releasing one of their players into running zone. The O player in the running zone is not allowed outside this area and must prevent the X player from running through the running zone and join the X players in the other end grid. If the ball goes out of the grid start again.

Ball Possession

Key Factors

TIME 40mins:

1. Keep close control of the ball.
2. Shield the ball while looking for a team player to pass to.
3. Create space to receive the ball while not in ball possession.
4. Team communicating with each other and be ready to receive the ball.

Equipment : Grids created from cones, 10 balls, bibs

Practice Sequence 1: 10 minutes The servers plays the ball to X1 or X2 who play to keep possession of the ball against defender O. The X players should attempt to score a goal in the small goal at one end.	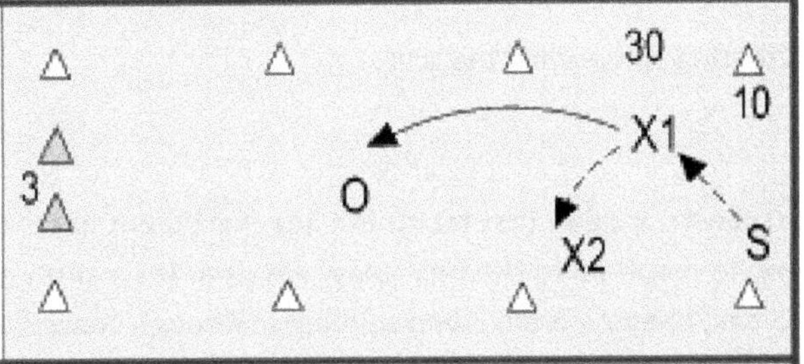 30 10 X1 O 3 X2 S
Practice Sequence 2: 10 minutes This is a 3 v 3 situation where both teams try to keep possession of the ball and attempt to score a goal. When the ball goes out of the grid, server 1 and 2 alternate playing the next ball into the grid area. Server 1 plays to the X players and server 2 to the O players.	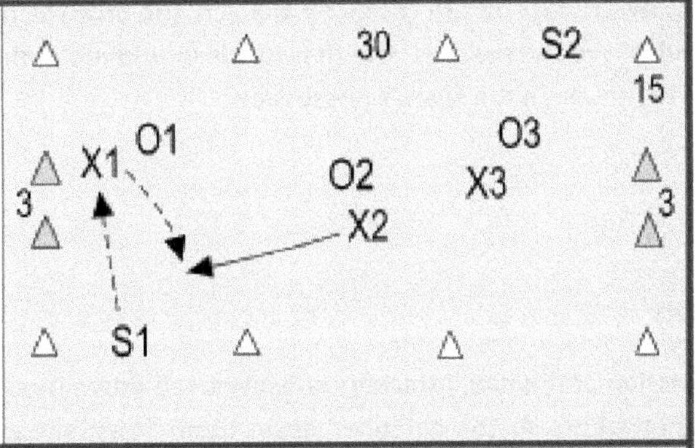 30 S2 15 X1 O1 O2 O3 X3 3 X2 3 S1
Practice Sequence 3: 20 minutes This is a 6 v 6 situation where both teams try to keep possession of the ball and attempt to score a goal. When the ball goes out of the grid, server 1 and 2 alternate playing the next ball into the grid area. Server 1 plays to the X players and server 2 to the O players.	S2 20 X1 O1 O5 X5 5 X2 O2 X4 O4 O6 X6 5 O3 X3 S1 40

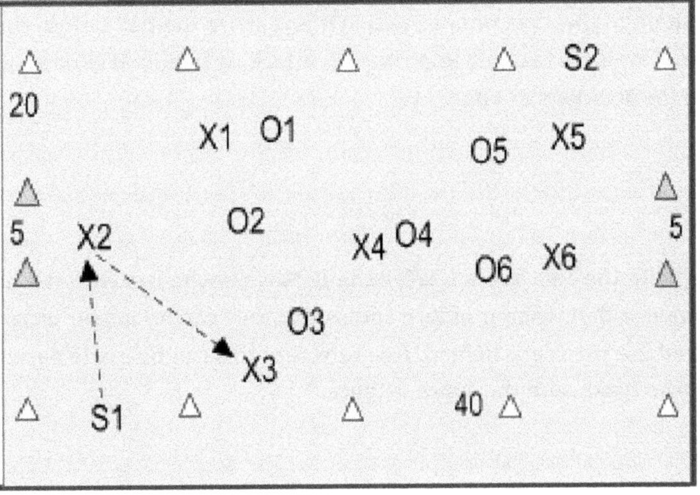

Creating Space

The ability of players to create space on the field is key to effective attacking play. Coaches play an important role in helping young players understand how to look for and create space. In this tutorial we will teach you 4 keys to creating space, and then give you some tips and drills to use to teach this important skill to your players.

Four Keys to Creating space with the ball

First Touch

Good ball control with a clean first touch is a key ingredient in creating space. The first touch allows the game to move on to the next play, whether it's a shot, dribble or pass. This means controlling the ball, keeping it alive and moving in enough space to make a decision and execute a play. Awareness before receiving will give the receiver the knowledge of where the defender is and where the space is. The first touch should move the player into the space and allow the ball to remain in the team's possession.

Draw Defenders

When in possession of the ball, attackers will be closed down by defenders, thus leaving space for supporting attackers. As the defender closes them down, the attacker must be aware of the space and position of their teammates within it and share the ball before the possibility to pass is closed down. This is particularly important in attacking overload situations where defenders can't cover all the attackers at once.

Turning

When running with the ball, space is left behind. Players who run with the ball should do so with the knowledge that when pressure comes and they can no longer progress, they can stop, turn around and use the space behind. Awareness of this can be made easier by doing a quick shoulder check to make sure the space is there.

Dribbling

Dribbling past defenders is an exciting part of the game but for the attacking team it is also means to create space. When an attacker beats a defender or two with a dribble, it unlocks the defensive strategy of the defending team by throwing them out of balance. This enables the attacking team to play in more time and space, often with overloads. The rewards for dribbling therefore are quite high.

Creatning Space As Individual

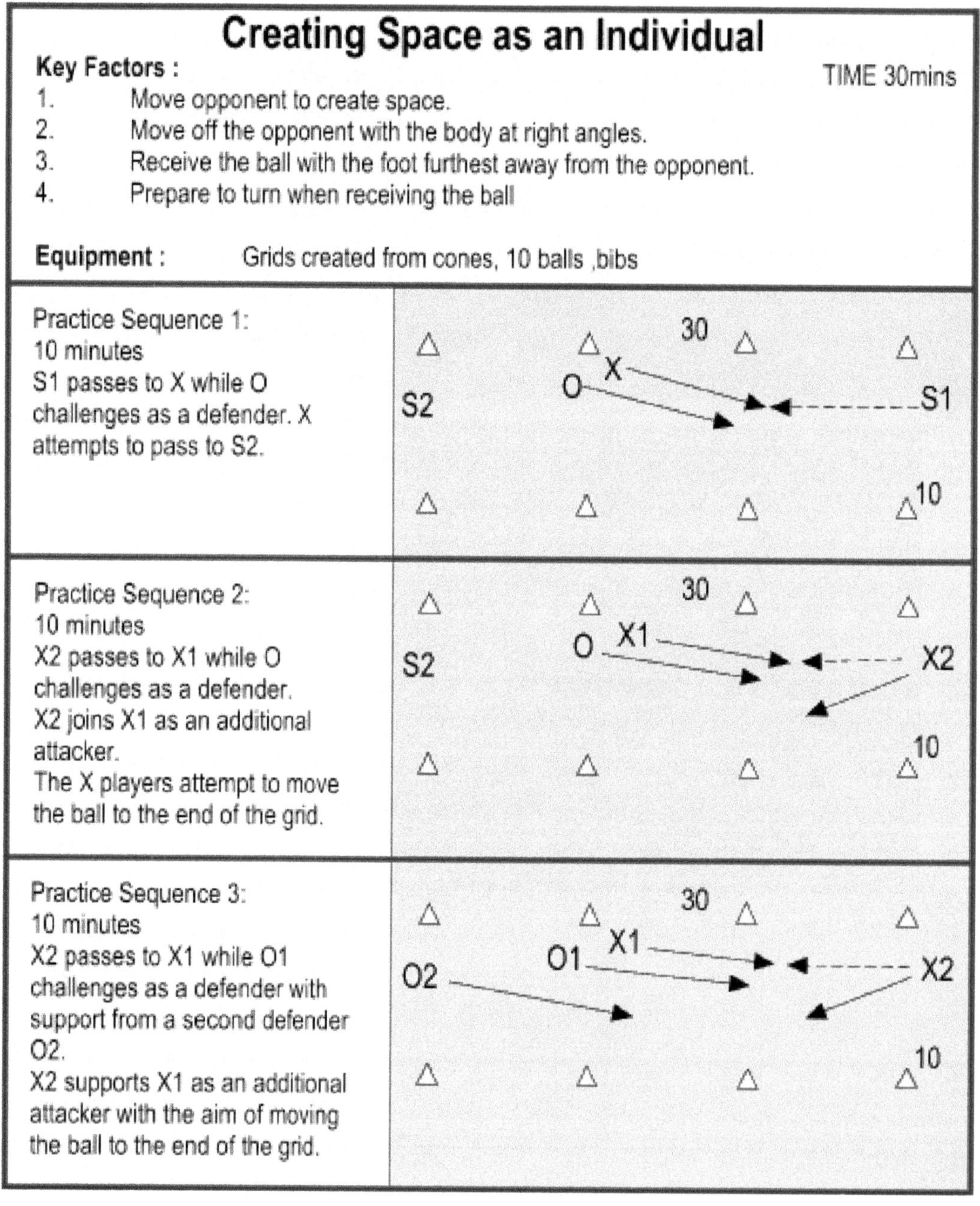

Creating Space as an Individual

TIME 30mins

Key Factors :

1. Move opponent to create space.
2. Move off the opponent with the body at right angles.
3. Receive the ball with the foot furthest away from the opponent.
4. Prepare to turn when receiving the ball

Equipment : Grids created from cones, 10 balls ,bibs

Practice Sequence 1: 10 minutes S1 passes to X while O challenges as a defender. X attempts to pass to S2.	30 X O S2 S1 10
Practice Sequence 2: 10 minutes X2 passes to X1 while O challenges as a defender. X2 joins X1 as an additional attacker. The X players attempt to move the ball to the end of the grid.	30 O X1 S2 X2 10
Practice Sequence 3: 10 minutes X2 passes to X1 while O1 challenges as a defender with support from a second defender O2. X2 supports X1 as an additional attacker with the aim of moving the ball to the end of the grid.	30 X1 O1 O2 X2 10

Creating Space with Wall Passes	
Key Factors : TIME 30mins 1. Player with the ball should run directly at the opponent. 2. The timing of the pass should draw the opponent to create space. 3. After passing, make a run into space behind the opponent. 4. The return pass should be in front of the attacking player. **Equipment :** Goal and penalty area , 10 balls , cones, bibs	
Practice Sequence 1: 15 minutes The server passes to X1. X2 runs to collect the pass from X1. X2 passes back to X1 who has made a run to into space. X3 runs to collect the pass from X1. X3 passes back to X1 who has made a run into the penalty area to shoot the ball.	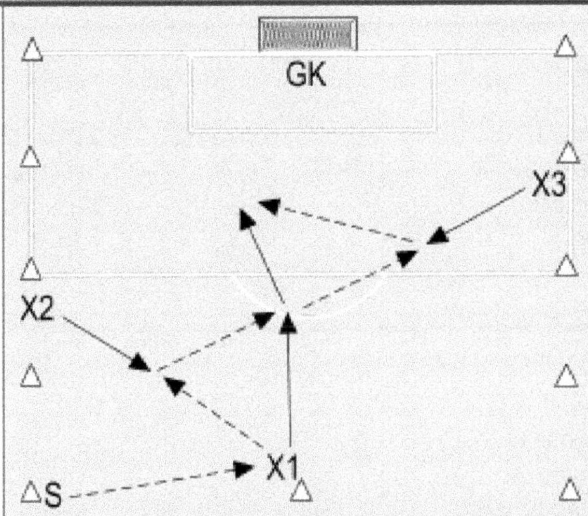
Practice Sequence 2: 15 minutes The server passes to X1. X2 runs to collect the pass from X1. X1 makes a run into space behind the defender O1 to collect the ball and shoot. X3 runs to create space for X1. Both O1 and O2 should defend to prevent a goal.	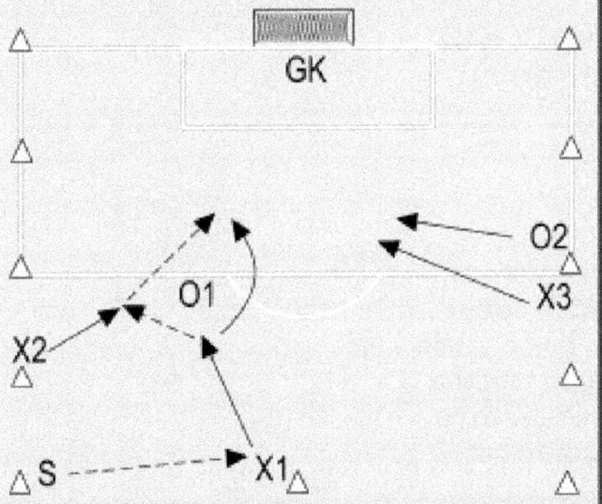

Creating Space as an Individual

Key Factors : TIME 30mins

1. Move opponent to create space.
2. Move off the opponent with the body at right angles.
3. Receive the ball with the foot furthest away from the opponent.
4. Prepare to turn when receiving the ball

Equipment : Grids created from cones, 10 balls ,bibs

Practice Sequence 1: 10 minutes S1 passes to X while O challenges as a defender. X attempts to pass to S2.	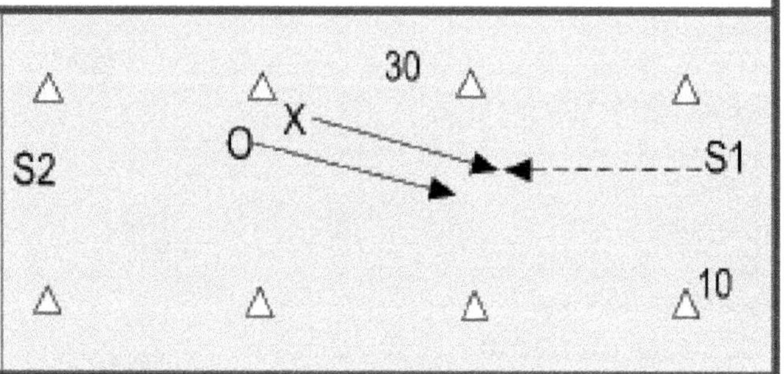 30 X O S2 S1 10
Practice Sequence 2: 10 minutes X2 passes to X1 while O challenges as a defender. X2 joins X1 as an additional attacker. The X players attempt to move the ball to the end of the grid.	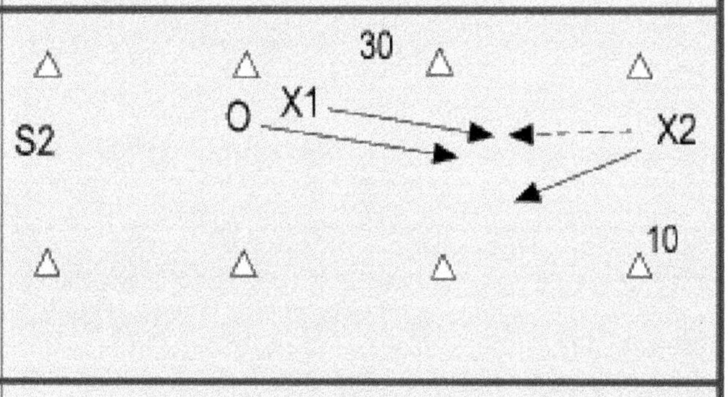 30 O X1 S2 X2 10
Practice Sequence 3: 10 minutes X2 passes to X1 while O1 challenges as a defender with support from a second defender O2. X2 supports X1 as an additional attacker with the aim of moving the ball to the end of the grid.	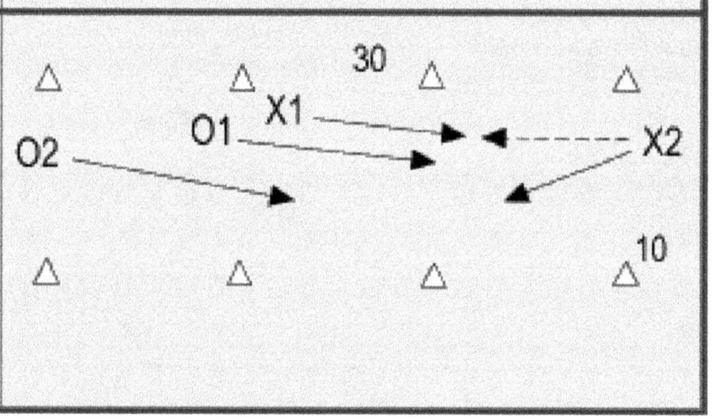 30 X1 O1 O2 X2 10

Creating Space by passing Inside

Key Factors :

TIME 30mins

1. Timing and accuracy of the pass.
2. Timing and accuracy of the runs.
3. Run inside of the player with the ball.
4. Receive the ball with body between opponent and the ball.

Equipment : Goal and penalty area , 10 balls , cones, bibs

Practice Sequence 1:
15 minutes
The server passes the ball to X1.
X2 runs to collect the pass from X1.
X2 then makes a run to score a goal. X1 runs forward to create space for X2.
Practice right and left.

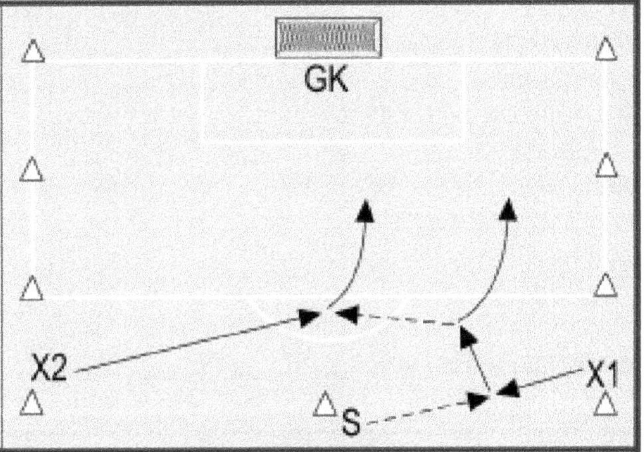

Practice Sequence 2:
15 minutes
X2 runs to collect the pass from the server.
X1 runs to collect the pass from X2.
X2 runs into the penalty area to collect the return pass from X1.
X2 makes a strike on goal while X1 creates space in the penalty area.
Practice right and left.
The O defenders should try to prevent the passes.

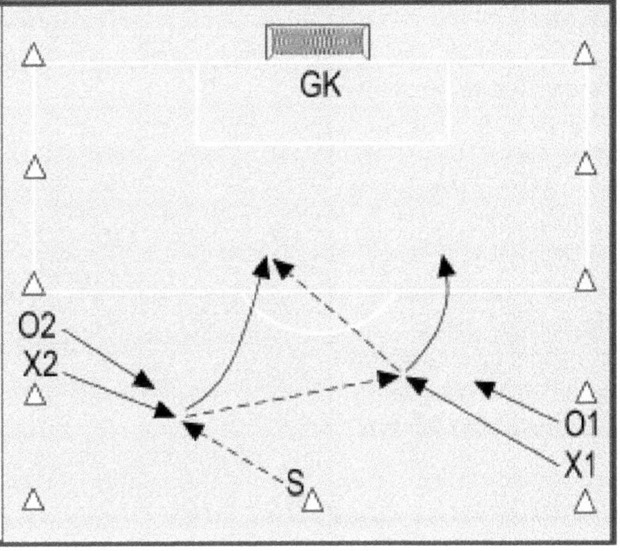

Creating Space in Attack

Key Factors : TIME 30mins

1. Create space to receive the ball.
2. Play the ball behind the defence and into the path of the receiving player.
3. Control the ball quickly and pass or make a one touch pass.
4. Always be prepared to receive the ball and be aware of the defence.

Equipment : Goal and penalty area , 10 balls , cones, bibs

Practice Sequence 1:
15 minutes
X3 runs to receive the ball from the server and then plays to X2 who comes to collect the ball.
X2 plays the ball into the path of X1 who makes a diagonal run to collect the ball.
X3 makes a run through the middle of the penalty area.
X1 should shoot to score a goal or pass to X3.
Alternate the starting point left and right.

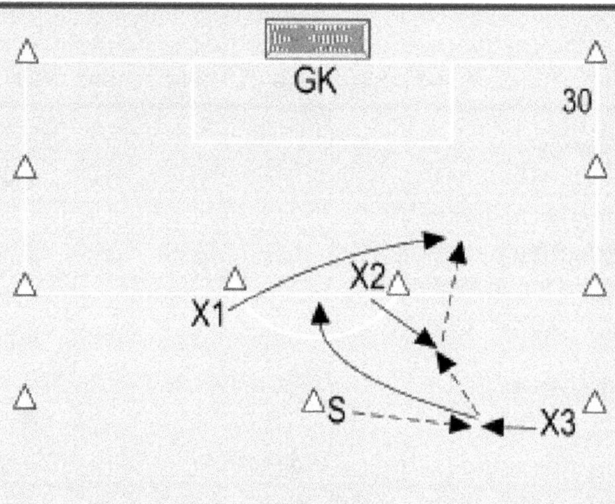

Practice Sequence 2:
15 minutes
X3 runs to receive the ball from the server and then plays to X2 who comes to collect the ball.
X2 can play the ball into the path of X1 or into the path of X3.
X1 or X3 should shoot to score a goal if possible or pass the ball off.
Both the defenders O1 and O2 should try to prevent the attackers from passing and scoring a goal.
Alternate the starting point left and right.

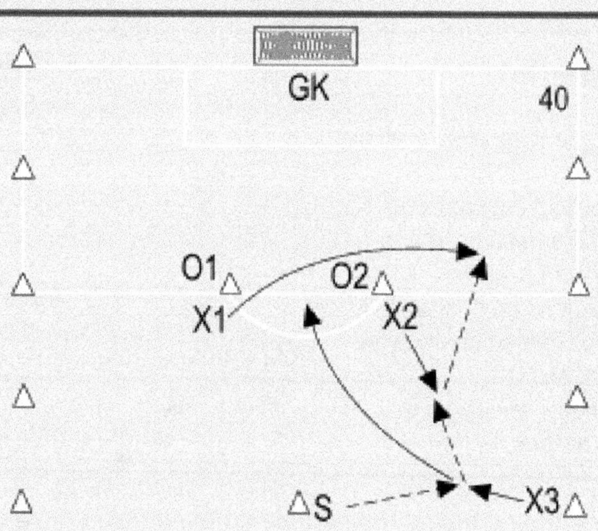

Creating Space

TIME 20mins

Key Factors :

1. Head up to view the play.
2. Run to the ball or into space away from or behind an opponent.
3. Timing and accuracy of the pass.
4. Speed of decisions.

Equipment : Small sided field 60 X 40 yards, 10 balls, bibs, cones

Starting Position :
X2 starts with the ball and make a pass to O6 and O6 then kicks the ball to the goalkeeper.
The goalkeeper throws the ball to X1.
Switch the start point between X1/O5/X2 and X2/O6/X1.

Practice Sequence :
When O5 has kicked the ball to the goalkeeper the practice is live.
The goalkeeper throws the ball to either X1 or X2 who should have created enough space to receive the ball.
All other X players should be prepared to receive the ball.

Overlap Running

Key Factors :

TIME 20mins

1. Run outside the player who was passed the ball.
2. Player communication.
3. Timing of the pass.
4. Run behind the opponent to create space.

Equipment : Small sided field 60 X 40 yards, 10 balls, bibs, cones

Starting Position :
X2 starts with the ball and makes a pass to O6 and O6 then kicks the ball to the goalkeeper.
The goalkeeper throws the ball to X2.
Switch the start point between X1/O5 and X2/O6.

Practice Sequence :
When O6 has kicked the ball to the goalkeeper the practice is live.
The goalkeeper throws the ball to X2 who should have created enough space to receive the ball.
X2 passes to X1 and makes an overlap run.
All other X players should be prepared to receive the ball.

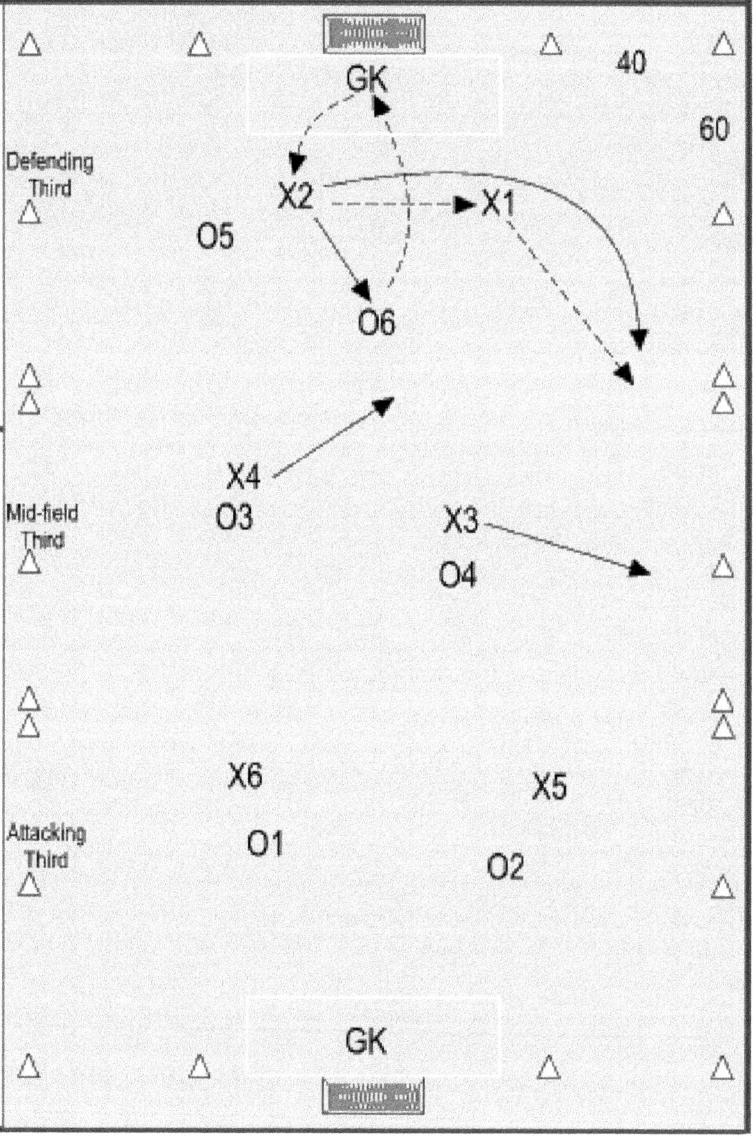

Diagonal Running

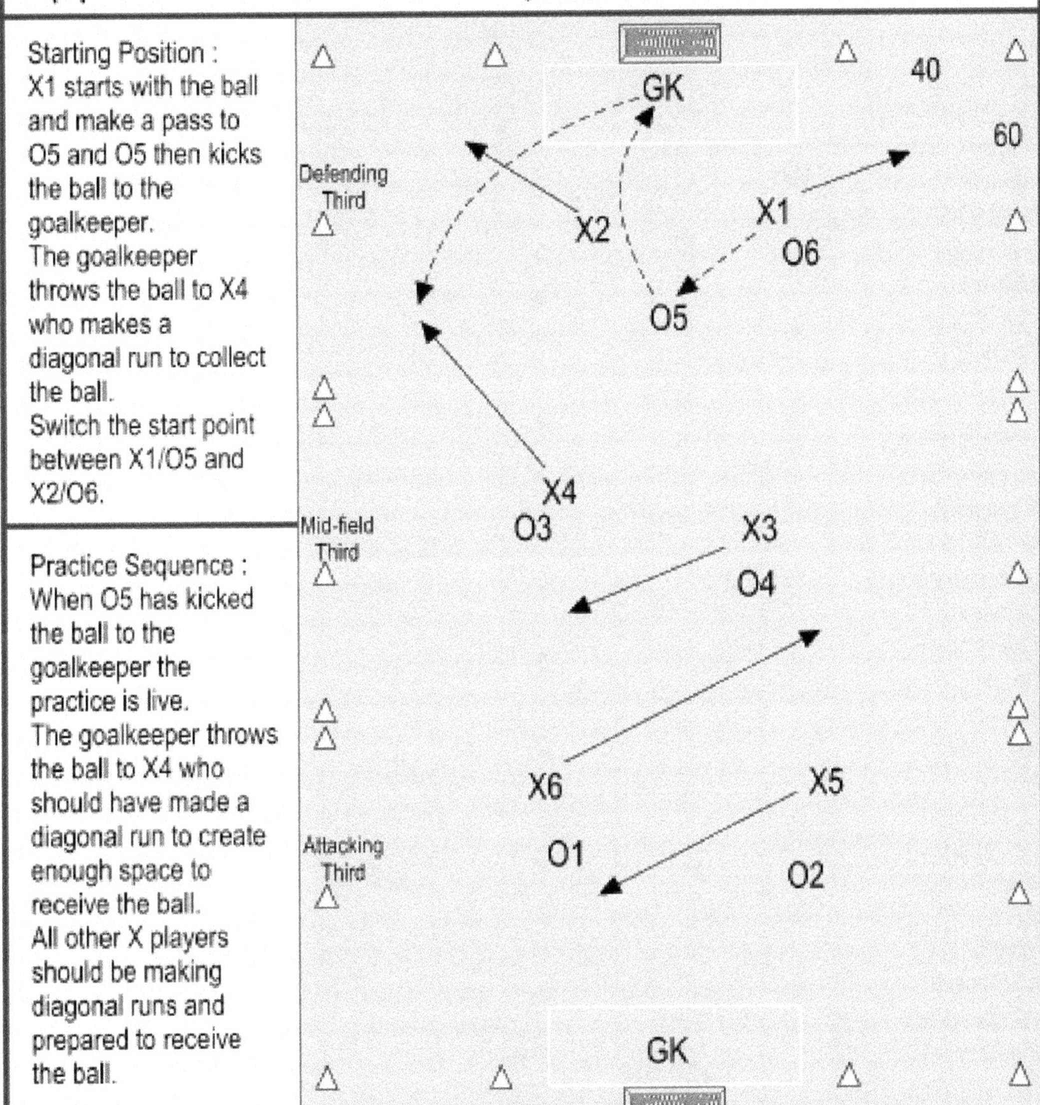

Diagonal Running

TIME 20mins

Key Factors :

1. Timing and accuracy of the pass and the pace on the ball.
2. Timing and angle of the runs.
3. Runs should be diagonal across the field.
4. Create space by running towards the ball or behind an opponent.

Equipment : Small sided field 60 X 40 yards, 10 balls, bibs, cones

Starting Position :
X1 starts with the ball and make a pass to O5 and O5 then kicks the ball to the goalkeeper.
The goalkeeper throws the ball to X4 who makes a diagonal run to collect the ball.
Switch the start point between X1/O5 and X2/O6.

Practice Sequence :
When O5 has kicked the ball to the goalkeeper the practice is live.
The goalkeeper throws the ball to X4 who should have made a diagonal run to create enough space to receive the ball.
All other X players should be making diagonal runs and prepared to receive the ball.

Create Width and length

Key Factors : TIME 20mins

1. Team with possession run wide and be ready to receive the ball.
2. Attackers run deep to draw the opposing defenders and create space.
3. Mid-field players run wide or deep depending on the space available.
4. All players run quickly and keep an eye on the player with the ball.

Equipment : Small sided field 60 X 40 created with cones, divided into thirds, 10 balls, bibs

Starting Position :
X2 passes to O6 who makes a lofted pass to the goalkeeper. The goalkeeper throws the ball to X1 and the play is live. Alternate between X2/O6 and X1/O5 to start the sequence.

Practice Sequence:
Coach the X players. All the players should create space from their respective defending players and be ready to receive the ball. The defenders should run wide and be ready to receive the ball. The mid-field players should create space from their defenders and be ready to receive the ball. The attacking players should create space to receive a long forward pass.

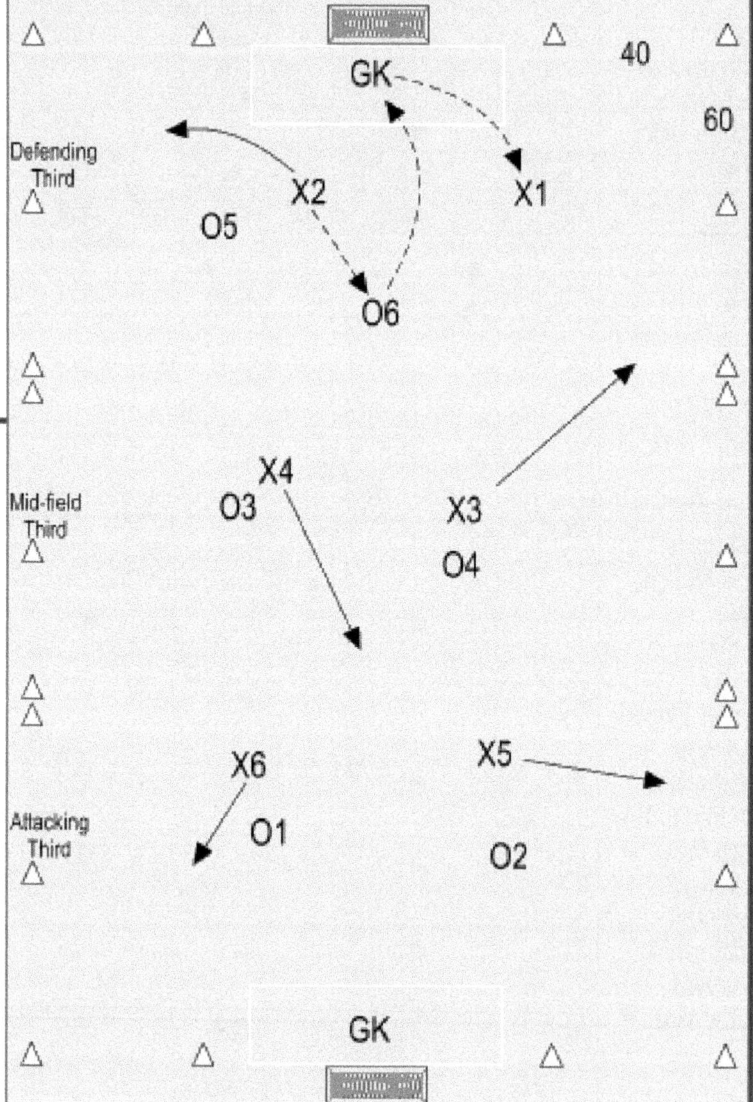

Attacking Principles

The five attacking principles

1 - penetration

2 - support

3 - depth

4 - mobility

5 - width

6 - creativity/improvisation

Penetration refers to getting inside and behind the defense's shape. Mobility is an offense's movement and flexibility, so its shape and direction are never predictable or repetitive.

Width is the ability of an offense to use the entire width of the field to spread out a defense and enable penetration or dangerous one-on-one isolation around the field. Creativity or improvisation are the offense's attacking freedom. As much as the principles is critical, following rote attacking directions make an offense easy to oppose. Improvisation allows attackers to express themselves, be unpredictable and find new ways to forge chances

Attacking 1 v 1

Attacking one on one with the Goalkeeper

Key Factors TIME 30mins:

1. Bring ball under control in front of the body and play it forward.
2. Check the position and movement of the goalkeeper.
3. Run at controlled speed.
4. Make decision to shoot or dribble.

Equipment : Goal and penalty area , 10 balls , cones, bibs

Practice Sequence 1:
15 minutes
Each X player takes turns in passing the ball to the server and runs into position to collect the ball.
The goalkeeper should close the angle of the attacker.
Keep a time limit of 10 seconds.

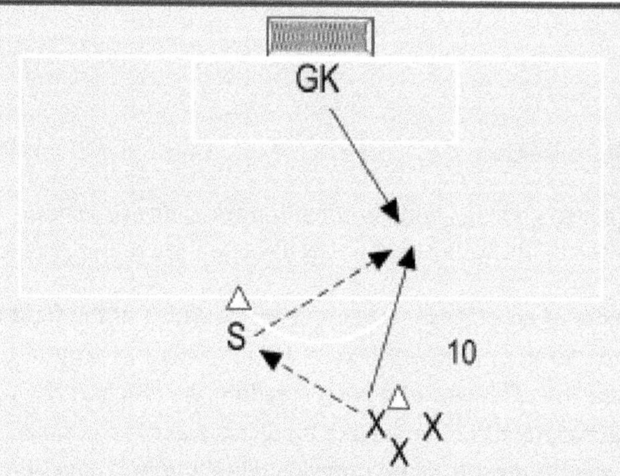

Practice Sequence 2:
15 minutes
The server passes the ball to X1.
The X players play the ball to free up one of the players to make a move toward the goal.
The defending O players are active as soon as the ball is played by the server to threaten the attackers.
Keep a time limit of 25 to 30 seconds.

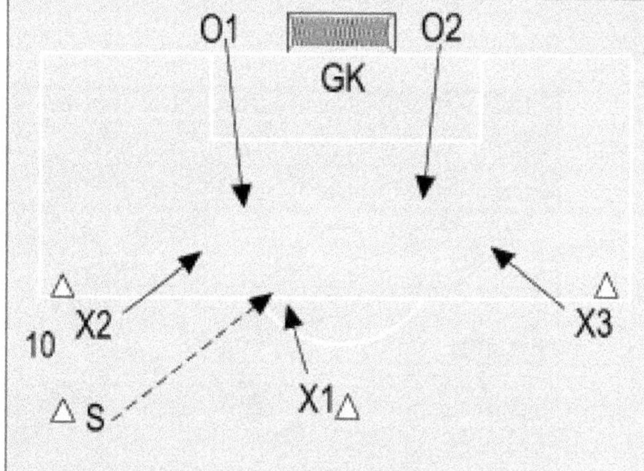

Ball Handling in an Attacking Position

Key Factors :

TIME 40mins

1. Keep your eye on the ball.
2. The body square to the incoming ball.
3. Have courage to attack the ball.
4. Decision on technique to use.

Equipment : Grids created from cones, 10 balls, bibs

Practice Sequence 1: 10 minutes The server throws the ball at head height to the X player who heads the ball to score a goal.	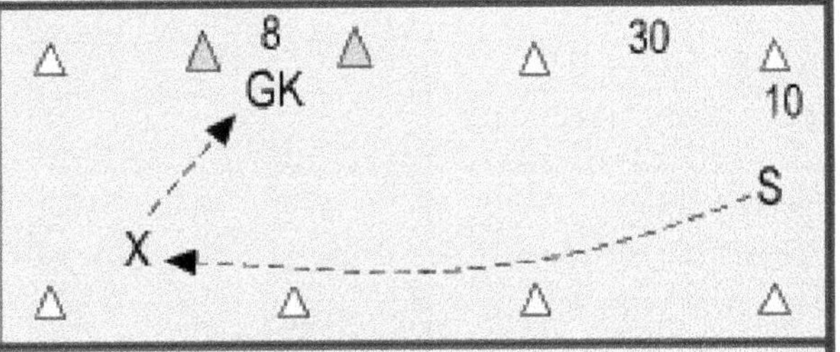
Practice Sequence 2: 10 minutes The server throws the ball to the X player who traps the ball with the chest and shoots first time with the foot.	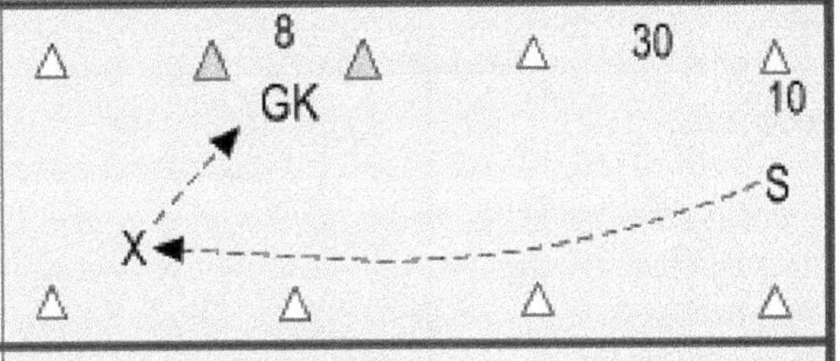
Practice Sequence 3: 10 minutes The server throws the ball at waist height to the X player who makes a diving header for shot on the goal.	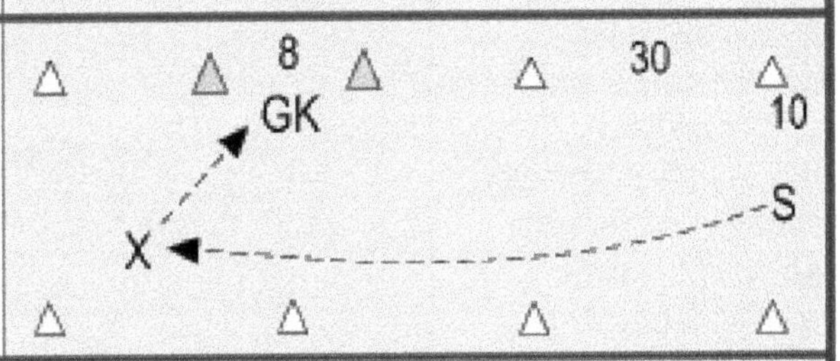
Practice Sequence 4: 10 minutes The server throws the ball to the X player who makes a decision which technique to use. The O player defends the goal.	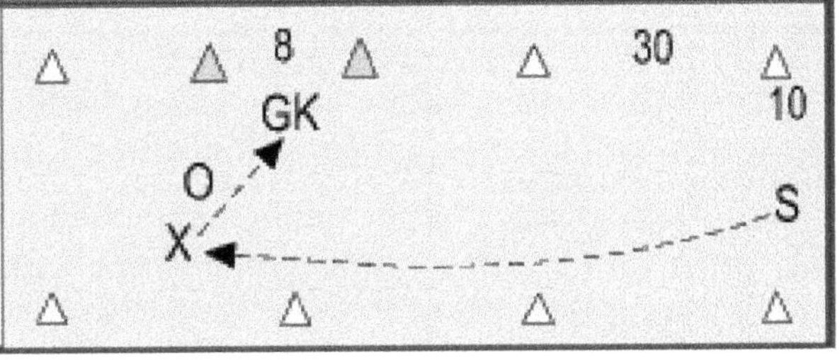

Dribbling in Attack

Key Factors :

TIME 30mins

1. Close control of the ball at all times.
2. Run at a controlled speed directly at the opponent.
3. Fake out the opponent, run quickly into the space created behind the opponent.
4. Keep good body balance.

Equipment : Goal and penalty area , 10 balls , cones, bibs

Practice Sequence 1:
10 minutes
Players from both the X and O teams take turns to dribble around and through the cones and pass the ball to the next player.
Players from the X and O teams should dribble at the same time to be an obstruction to each other.

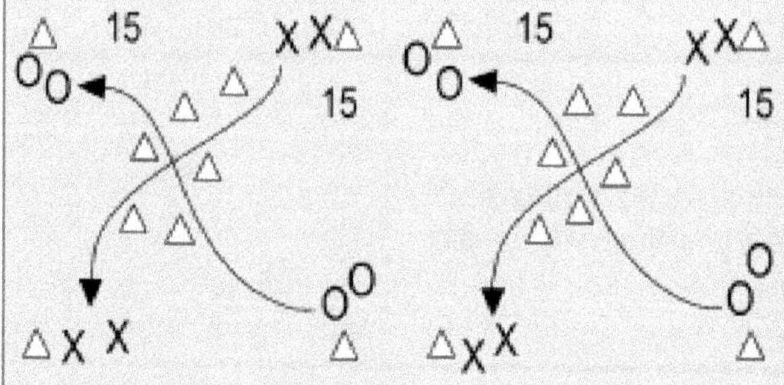

Practice Sequence 2:
10 minutes
The X player passes the ball to the server and runs into the grid area to receive the returned pass.
The X player then proceeds to dribble through the cones and the O players, for a shot on goal.
The 5 O defenders must keep one foot on the cone but can use the other foot to defend the area.
Alternating starting left and right.

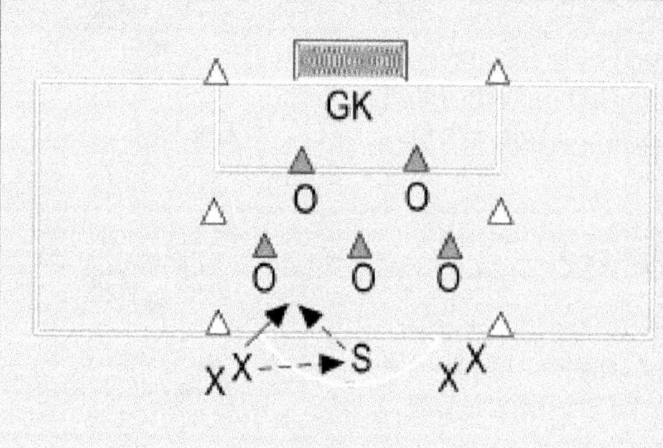

Practice Sequence 2:
10 minutes
The 3 O defending players should prevent an X player from scoring a goal.
The X players pass the ball around until one of the players has enough space to dribble towards the goal to take a shot.

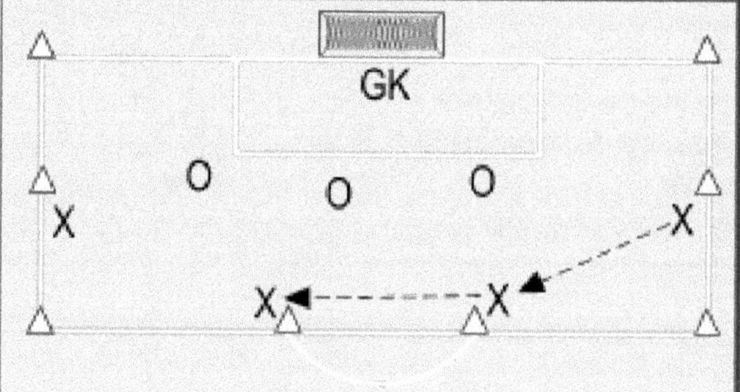

Attacking across the Penalty Area

TIME 30mins

Key Factors :

1. Run to the end line and pass back across the penalty area.
2. Attacking players make curved runs across the goal.
3. Timing of the pass and run across the penalty area.
4. Be first to the ball and get in front of the defence.

Equipment : Goal and penalty area, 10 balls, bibs , cones

Practice Sequence 1:
10 minutes
X1 passes to X2 and runs outside the cones towards the end of the grid to receive the return pass from X2.
X1 runs with the ball to the end of the grid and passes the ball back to X2 who has run into position to receive the pass and shoot.

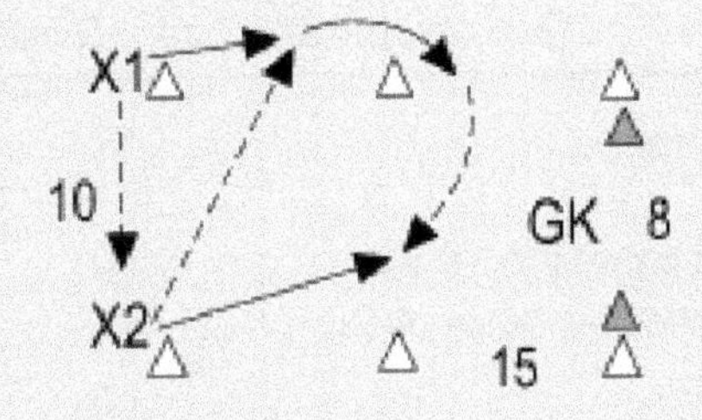

Practice Sequence 2:
10 minutes
X1 passes to X2 and runs outside the cones towards the end line to receive the return pass from X2.
X1 runs with the ball to the end line and passes the ball back across the penalty area for X2 or X3 to attack the goal.
Alternate starting left and right side of the penalty area.

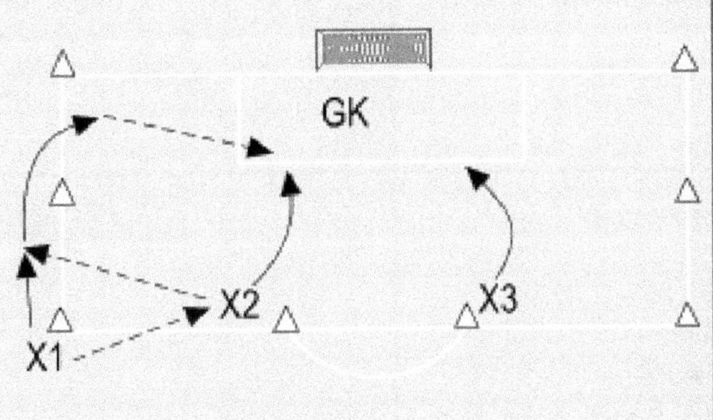

Practice Sequence 3:
10 minutes
X1 passes to X2 and runs outside the cones towards the end line to receive the return pass from X2.
X1 runs with the ball to the end line and passes the ball back across the penalty area for X2 or X3 to attack the goal.
O1 and O2 should defend the goal.
Alternate starting left and right side of the penalty area.

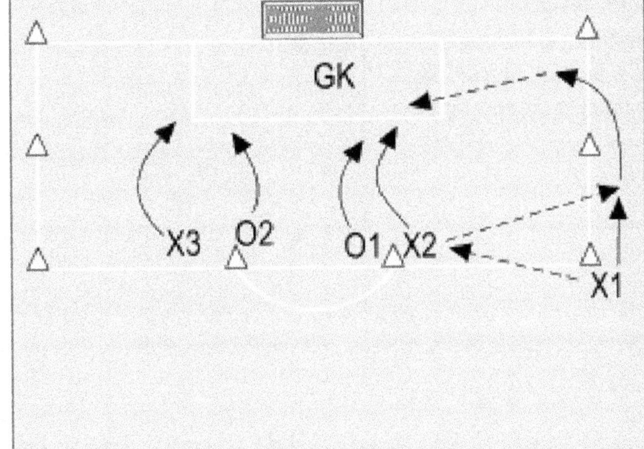

Diagonal Passing and Running in Attack

Key Factors : TIME 30mins

1. Timing and accuracy of the pass and pace on the ball.
2. Timing and angle of the runs.
3. Runs should be diagonal and across the field.
4. Create space by running to the ball or behind an opponent.

Equipment : Goal and penalty area , 10 balls , cones, bibs

Practice Sequence 1:
15 minutes
The X1 player passes to X2 and makes a diagonal run between the cones.
X2 passes the ball to X1 outside of the cones and then makes a diagonal run outside the opposite cone.

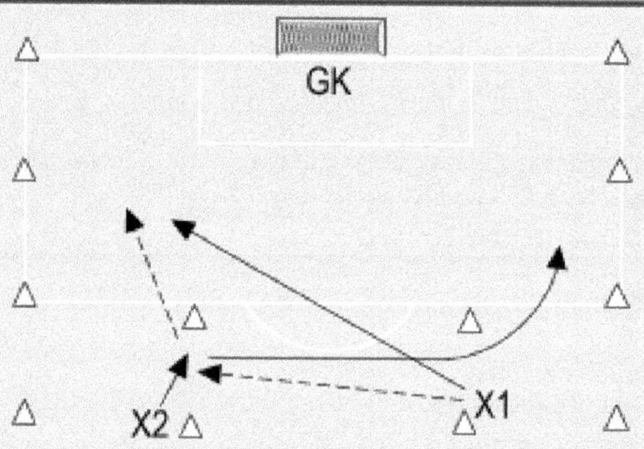

Practice Sequence 2:
15 minutes
X1 receives a pass from the server and passes to X2. X2 runs to receive the pass and passes to X3 and makes a diagonal run to the outside.
X3 runs to receive the pass from X2 and attacks the goal.
The two defenders O1 and O2 threaten the attacking players as soon as the pass is played by the server.

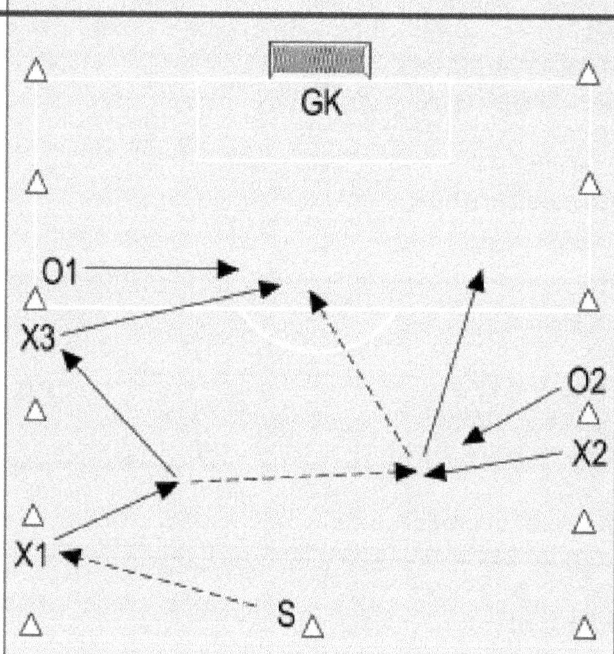

Attacking in and around the Penalty Area

Key Factors :

TIME 30mins

1. Create space.
2. Make an early decision shoot, dribble or pass.
3. Attack the back of the defence.
4. Timing and accuracy of the passes.

Equipment : Goal and penalty area , 10 balls , cones, bibs

Practice Sequence 1: 15 minutes
The goalkeeper passes the ball to X1 and when X1 touches the ball the practice is live.
X2 and X3 join X1 in the attack while O1 and O2 defend the area.

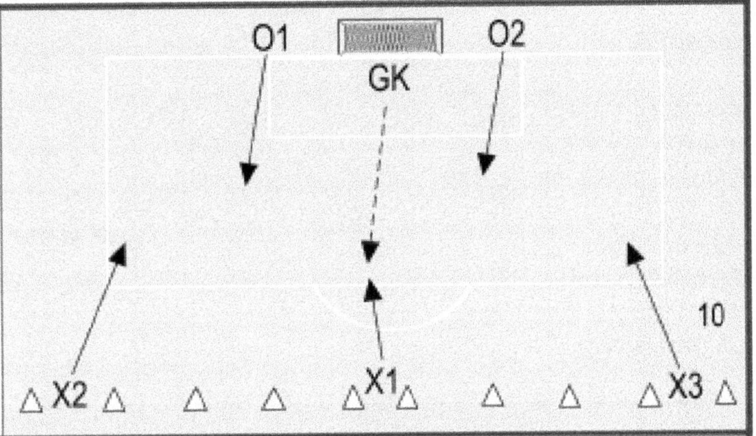

Practice Sequence 2: 15 minutes
The goalkeeper throws the ball to X1 and when X1 touches the ball, the practice is live.
X2, X3 and X4 join X1 in the attack while O1, O2 and O3 defend the area giving a 4 v 3 situation with the attackers having the numerical advantage.

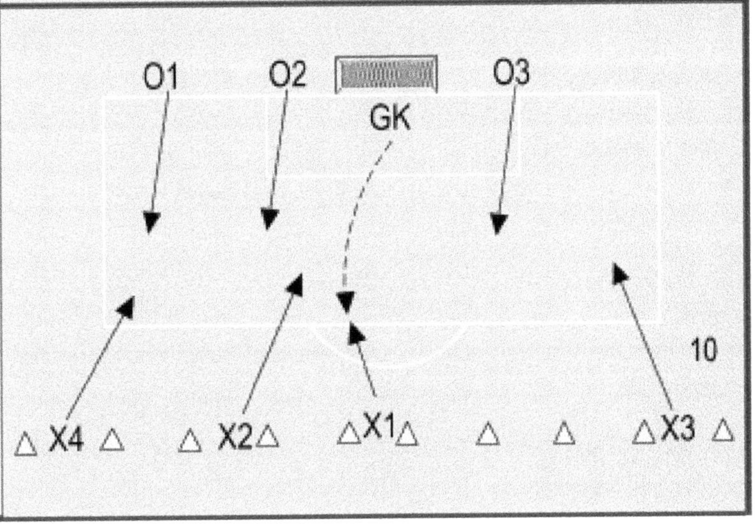

Attacking Inside the Penalty Area

Key Factors :

TIME 30mins

1. Create space to receive the ball.
2. Turn and receive the ball in one move and shoot at first opportunity.
3. Get in front of the defender and be first to the ball.
4. Supporting player runs to create space to receive the ball.

Equipment : Goal and penalty area, 10 balls, bibs , cones

Practice Sequence 1:
10 minutes
Number the servers 1 through 3.
The X player calls a server's number and runs to collect the ball.
The X player has only two touches of the ball to bring it under control and shoot.
Change out X players after 6 consecutive balls.

20
GK
S2
X
S1
S1

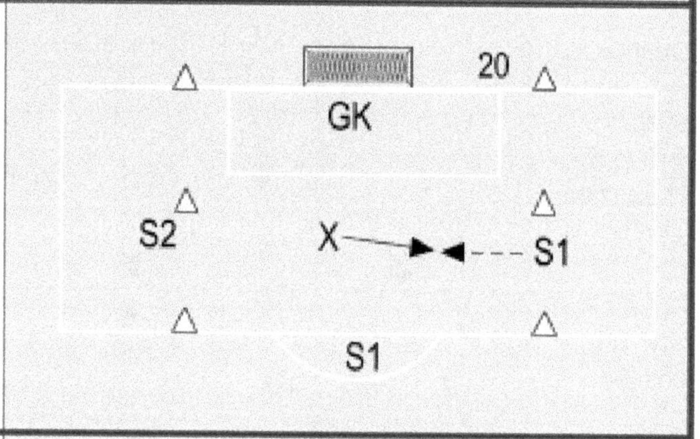

Practice Sequence 2:
10 minutes
Number the servers 1 through 3.
The X player calls a server's number and runs to collect the ball.
The defender should prevent X from scoring a goal.
Change out X players after 6 consecutive balls.

20
GK
O
S2
X
S1
S1

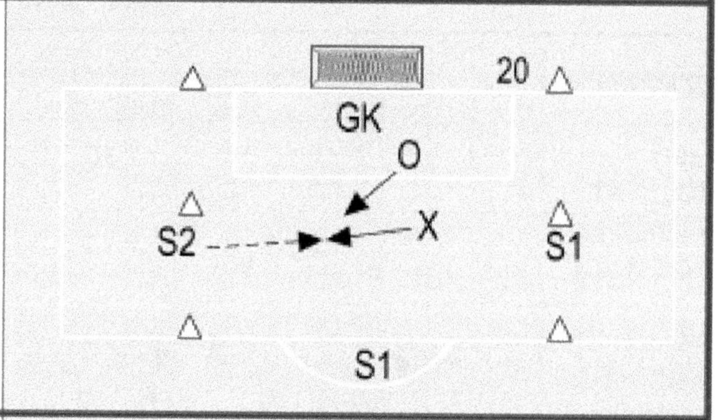

Practice Sequence 3:
10 minutes
The servers S1 and S2 should alternately put the ball into play.
The servers can play the ball anywhere inside the penalty area.
X1 and X2 should run to receive the ball and score against defenders O1 and O2.

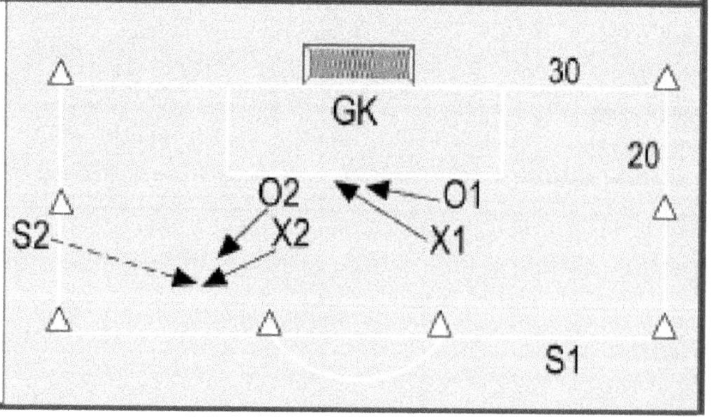

30
GK
20
O2
O1
S2
X2
X1
S1

Running and Passing at Close Angles

Key Factors : TIME 30mins

1. Control the ball with first touch, a ground pass with the second touch.
2. Pass the ball into space in front of the receiving player.
3. Accuracy and timing of the pass.
4. The body should be over the ball and played with pace.

Equipment : Goal and penalty area , 10 balls , cones, bibs

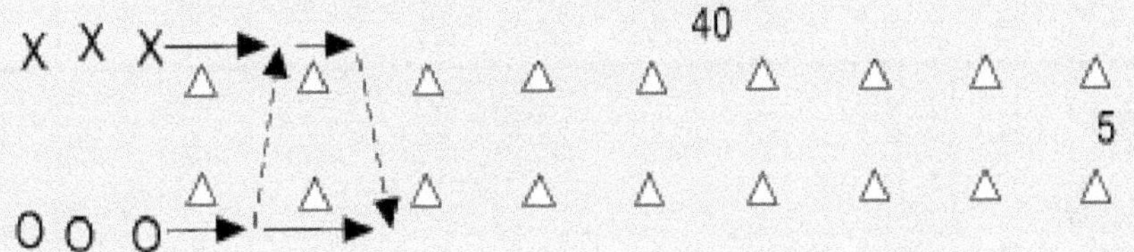

Practice Sequence 1: 10 minutes
The O and X players run alone the outside of the cones and make diagonal passes across the grid. When the players reach the end of the grid they run back outside the grid with the ball to the beginning.

Practice Sequence 2:
10 minutes
The server makes a pass to X1 who controls the ball and passes immediately to the oncoming X2 player.
X3 makes a run into the middle of the penalty area to receive the direct pass from X2.
X3 should take a direct shot on the goal.
Alternate starting left and right.

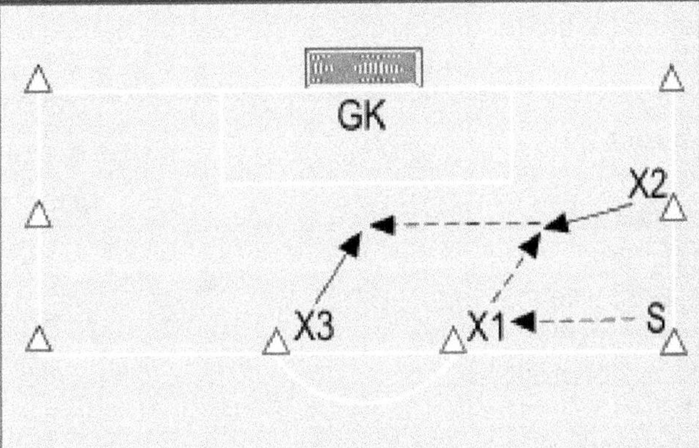

Practice Sequence 3:
10 minutes
The server makes a pass to X1 who controls the ball and passes immediately to the oncoming X2 player.
X3 makes a run into the middle of the penalty area to receive the direct pass from X2.
X3 can make a direct shot on goal or pass to X1 who has made an overlap run behind the defence.
Alternate starting left and right.

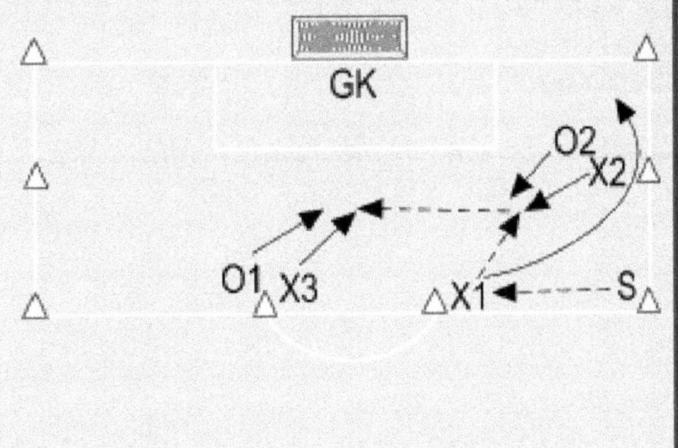

Attacking the Ball around the Goal

Key Factors :

TIME 30mins

1. Be first to the ball.
2. Receive the ball and turn in one movement.
3. Control the ball and shoot around opponents.
4. Move in one direction, check and move away from the opponent.

Equipment : Goal and penalty area , 10 balls , cones, bibs

Practice Sequence 1:
15 minutes
S1 makes a lofted pass into the penalty area alternating with S2 who makes a throw-in into the penalty area, but not at the same time.
The 3 X players make an attacking play on the ball to score a goal.

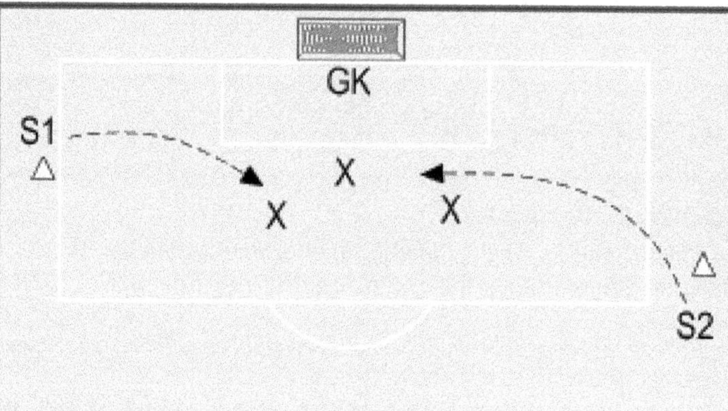

Practice Sequence 2:
15 minutes
S1 makes a lofted pass into the penalty area alternating with S2 who makes a throw-in into the penalty area, but not at the same time.
The 4 X players make an attacking play on the ball to score a goal while the 2 O players defend the goal, supporting the goalkeeper

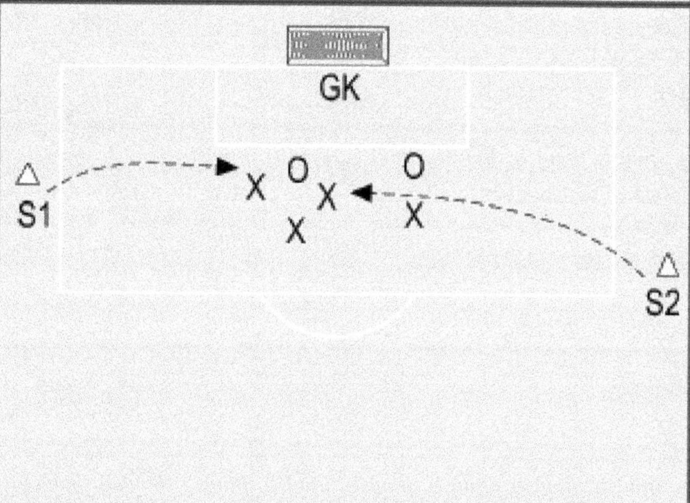

Defending

Attacking wins games. Defending wins championships

The importance of a quality defense cannot be overlooked. Defending is the cornerstone of every team and should be one of your teams main focuses if you are serious about winning Soccer games. It is very difficult for the opposition to beat you, if they can't score on you.

If you are one of those players who thinks your are too good to defend. Well if that's the case you are probably not reading this post. But if you are, please take your left hand, and slap yourself in the face. Everyone on the team has to defend! That's the key to proper defending.

!

Moving on...

If you take a look at all the professional teams, one common trait in all of the top clubs is their ability to defend. You don't see teams winning titles and cups, simply by scoring more goals than the other team. The foundation of these teams is their ability to shut down their opposition on the defensive end.

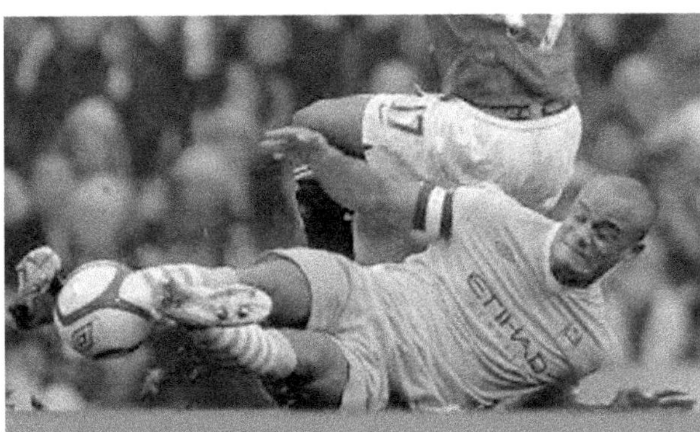

In order for your team to establish itself as a powerful defensive soccer presence, you will have to spend a significant amount of time working on your defensive shape. Holding strong defensive soccer shape is the act of a team defending as a whole.

Defending starts from the strikers and continues all the way back to the goalkeeper. Everyone on the team is responsible for defending and must put in the work required if you want to be able to reduce the amount of goals your team concedes. I know, I know. Most players are not

too excited when it comes to defending and may not always give their full effort. But this mentality needs to be changed immediately. Defending is a major component of Soccer and when you learn to properly close down the opposition and win the ball, defending can be a lot of fun.

Defensive soccer shape is not something that can happen based solely on individual talents. In order for a team to become defensively organized, a lot of practice will have to take place.

Like all sports, soccer has developed its contemporary tactical systems through generations of evolution. Although they may not be definitive, that the five principles of attacking and defending were put to paper and submitted officially in a book endorsed by the highest soccer governing body in England gives the principles a credibility that led to a central role in any discussion of tactics or coaching strategy in the sport.

Defending Turning and Support

TIME 30mins

Key Factors :

1. Be patient and watch the ball.
2. Prevent the opponent from turning with the ball.
3. Select the correct moment to tackle.
4. Steer the opponent towards the supporting player or the side line.

Equipment : Grids created from cones, 10 balls, bibs

Practice Sequence 1: 10 minutes S1 passes to X while O challenges as a defender. X attempts to pass to S2.	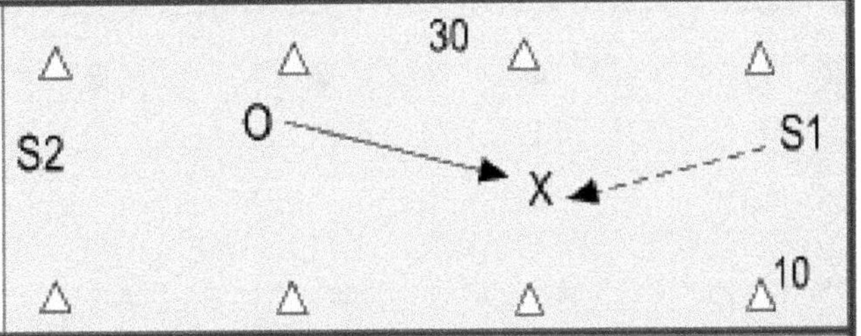 30 O S1 S2 X 10
Practice Sequence 2: 10 minutes S1 passes to X while O1 challenges as a defender with support from a second defender O2. X attempts to move the ball to the end of the grid.	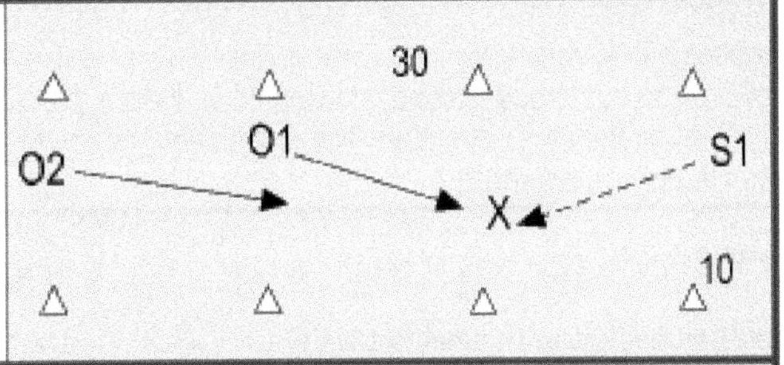 30 O1 S1 O2 X 10
Practice Sequence 3: 10 minutes X2 passes to X1 while O1 challenges as a defender with support from a second defender O2. X2 supports X1 as an additional attacker, with the aim to move the ball to the end of the grid.	30 O1 X2 O2 X1 10

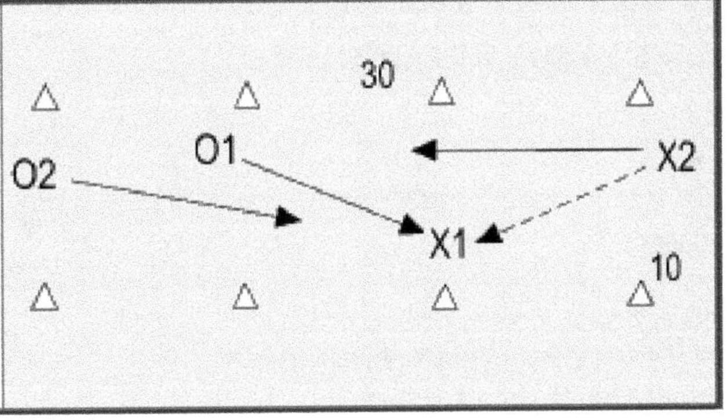

Defending by Marking Players

Key Factors : TIME 30mins

1. Travel quickly when the ball is played to the opponent to be defended.
2. Slow down when closing in on the opponent.
3. Prevent the ball being played forward.
4. Recover defensive position when the ball is played.

Equipment : Grids created from cones, 10 balls ,bibs

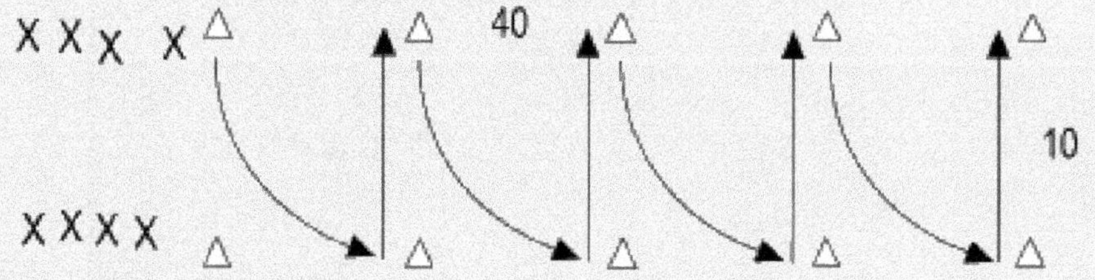

Practice Sequence 1: 10 minutes
Run in a half circle to the opposite cone, slowing down before the cone. Side skip to the cone opposite, facing the same direction. The first player goes right, the second player left, and alternate the players around.

Practice Sequence 2:
10 minutes
The X players can pass to each other but the O players must prevent either of the X players from shooting at one of the goals at the furthest end of the grid.

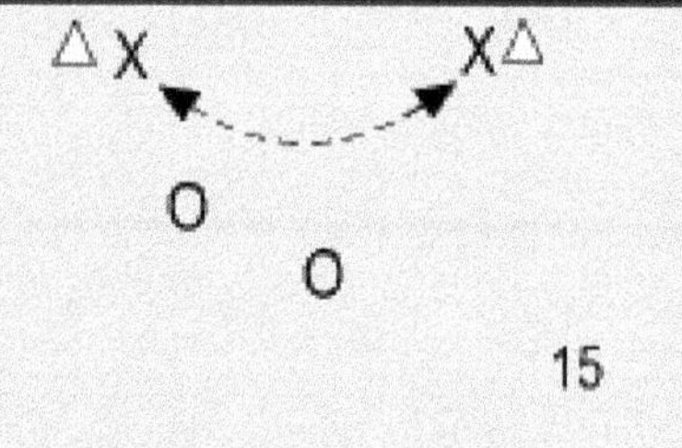

Practice Sequence 3:
10 minutes
The X players can pass to each other but the O players must prevent either of the X players from passing forward to the forward X player.
The forward X player can move from side to side to receive the ball.

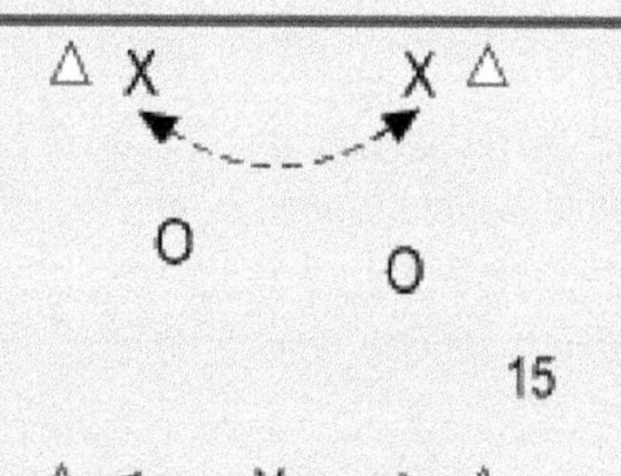

Prevent Opponents from Turning

Key Factors : TIME 30mins

1. Close down the space quickly between defender and opponent.
2. Keep goal side of the ball and be patient.
3. Be close enough to prevent the opponent from turning.
4. Steer opponent to the supporting player.

Equipment : Goal and penalty area, 10 balls, bibs , cones

Practice Sequence 1: 15 minutes The servers take turns in passing the ball to either X1 or X2. The X player should run to receive the ball from the server. The other X player should create space to receive the ball. The players should only play in the grid area and if the ball goes out the server should play another ball.	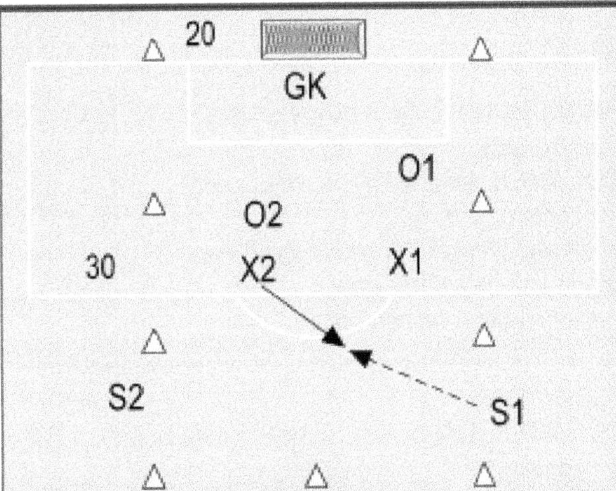
Practice Sequence 2: 15 minutes The servers take turns in passing the ball to either X1, X2 or X3. The X player should run to receive the ball from the server. The other 2 X players should create space to receive the ball. The players should only play in the grid area and if the ball goes out the server should play another ball.	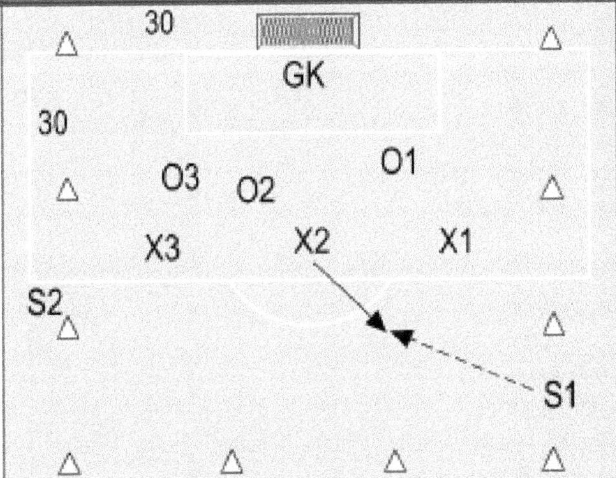

Defending and Supporting in the Penalty Area

Key Factors : TIME 30mins

1. Travel quickly when the ball is played to the opponent to be defended.
2. Slow down when closing in on the opponent.
3. Prevent the ball being played forward.
4. Recover defensive position when the ball is played.

Equipment : Goal and penalty area , 10 balls , cones, bibs

Practice Sequence 1:
10 minutes
The server passes the ball to the X player on the opposite side of the grid.
The 2 X players should play the ball between them and attempt to score a goal.
The O defenders should start the sequence in the middle of the grid and defend the goal.
Alternate the starting between servers.

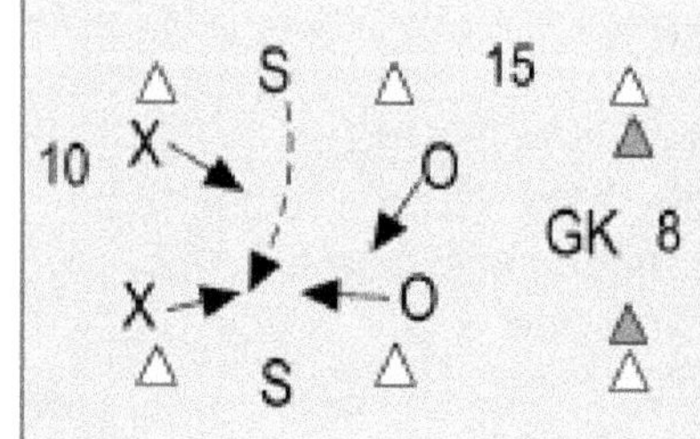

Practice Sequence 2:
10 minutes
To start either server S1 passes the ball to X1 or server S2 passes to X2.
The 2 O players defend against the X players to prevent a goal being scored.
The sequence stops when the ball goes out of the penalty area.

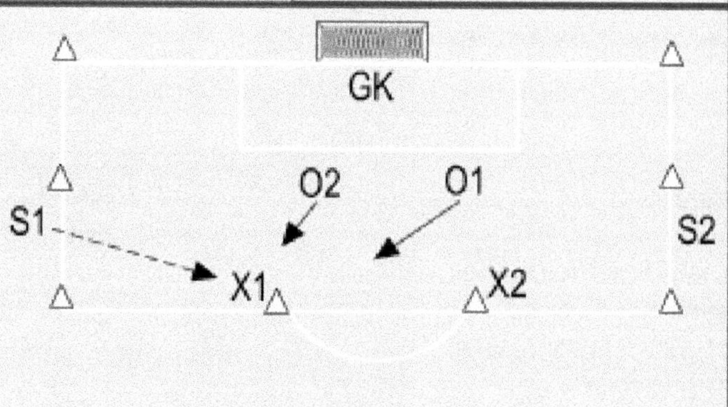

Practice Sequence 3:
10 minutes
Start with either server S1 passing the ball to X1 or server S2 passing to X2.
The O players defend against the X players to prevent a goal being scored.
The sequence stops when the ball goes out of the penalty area.

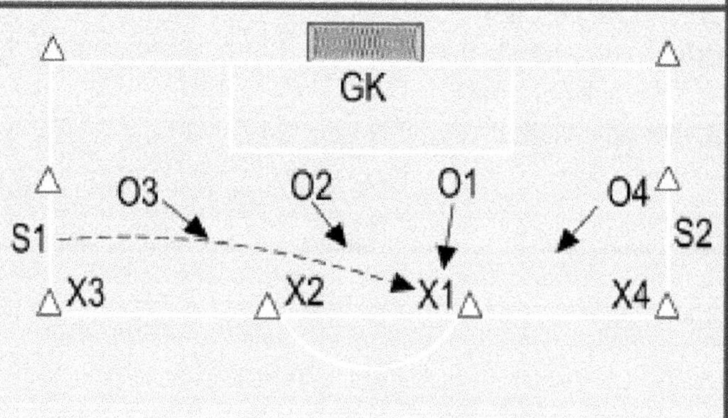

Defending around the Penalty Area

TIME 30mins

Key Factors :

1. Close down the opponent quickly.
2. Prevent opponent from turning.
3. Steer opponent towards the supporting player and or the side line.
4. Supporting player position.

Equipment : Goal and penalty area , 10 balls , cones, bibs

Practice Sequence 1:
15 minutes
The goalkeeper kicks the ball out to an X player.
The O player defends against the X player.

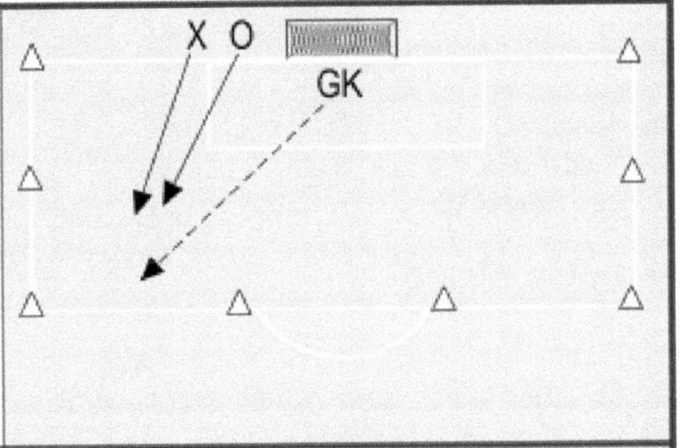

X O
GK

Practice Sequence 2:
15 minutes
The goalkeeper kicks the ball out to one of the X players. Both of the O players defend against the X players.
The X players work as a team to attack the goal while the O players defend as a team.

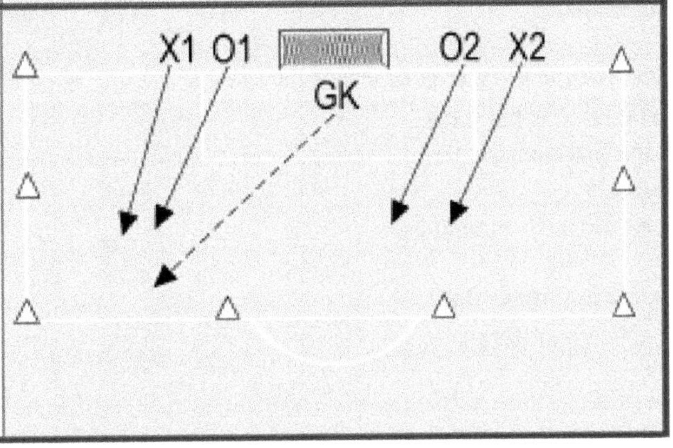

X1 O1 O2 X2
GK

Defending Against Opponents Facing the Goal

Key Factors :

TIME 30mins

1. Close the space down quickly between defender and attacker.
2. Make a curved run the show direction to steer opponent.
3. Shuffle last 2 steps with the leading foot outside of the line of the ball.
4. Support player angle and position.

Equipment : Goal and penalty area , 10 balls , cones, bibs

Practice Sequence 1:
15 minutes
The X player passes the ball to the server who passes between the X player and the defender O.
The X player should receive the ball first and should attempt to score a goal.
Alternate the play both right and left.

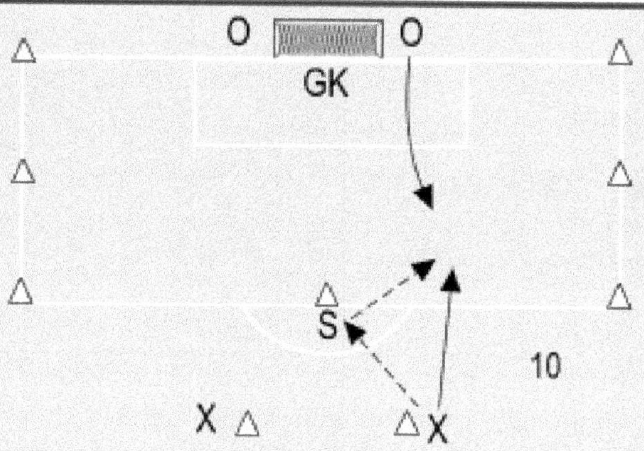

Practice Sequence 2:
15 minutes
The X2 player passes the ball to the server who returns the pass.
X2 controls the ball and dribbles towards the goal.
The O2 player defends against the X2 player.
O1 supports O2 but tracks the position X1 who also attacks.

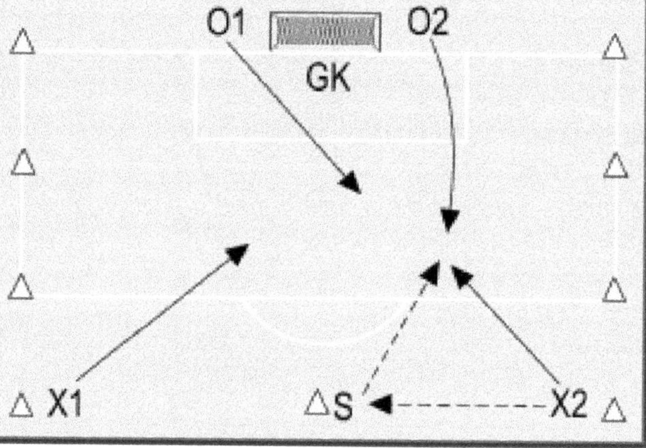

Tracking and Marking Players

Key Factors : TIME 30mins

1. Close opponent down quickly.
2. Keep goal side of the ball.
3. Force opponent across the field.
4. Keep ball and opponent in view.

Equipment : Goal and penalty area , 10 balls , cones, bibs

Practice Sequence 1:
15 minutes
The server passes the ball to X who dribbles towards the goal. The O player defends against the X player.

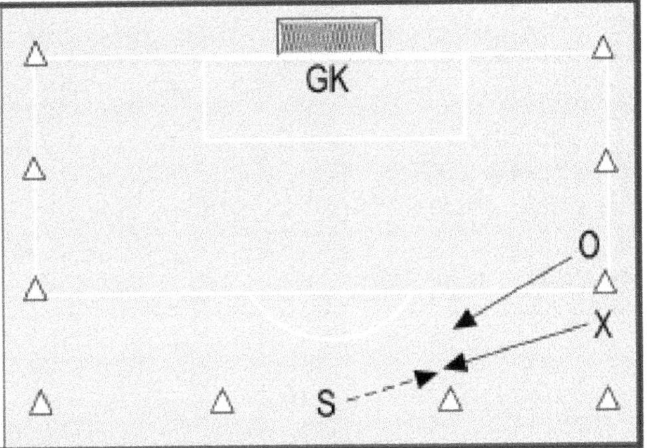

GK
O
X
S

Practice Sequence 2:
15 minutes
The server passes the ball to X1 who dribbles towards the goal with the assistance of attacker X2 . O1 and O2 should defend the penalty area creating a 2 v 2 situation.

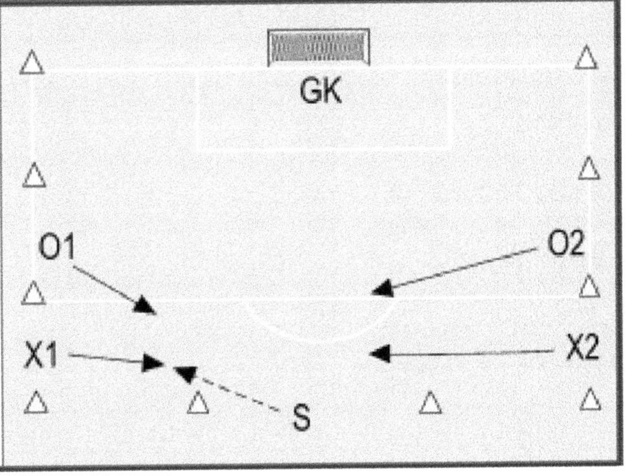

GK
O1
O2
X1
X2
S

Defending the Penalty Area

Key Factors :

TIME 30mins

1. Move to the ball first and attack it at its highest trajectory.
2. Play the ball clear of the attacking player.
3. Play the ball in the opposite direction from which it came.
4. Move out of the penalty area after clearing.

Equipment : Goal and penalty area , 10 balls , cones, bibs

Practice Sequence 1:
15 minutes
The server plays the ball to X1 or X2 who makes a cross into the penalty area.
The O players should play the ball out of the penalty area.

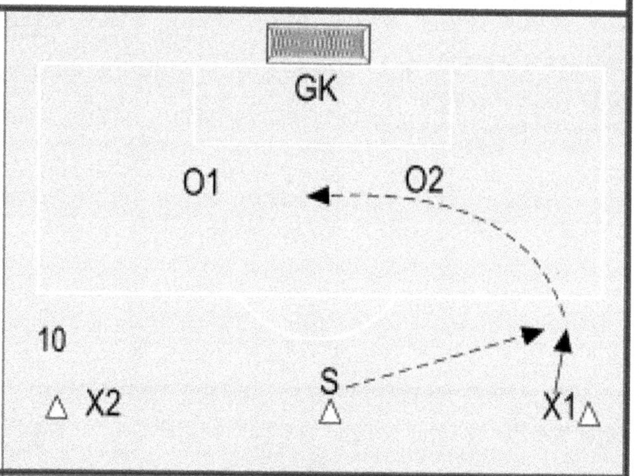

GK
O1
O2
10
X2
S
X1

Practice Sequence 2:
15 minutes
The server passes the ball to X1 or X2 who take it in turn to cross the ball into the penalty area.
O1, O2 and O3 should defend the penalty area with the goalkeeper, while X3 and X4 attempt to score a goal.

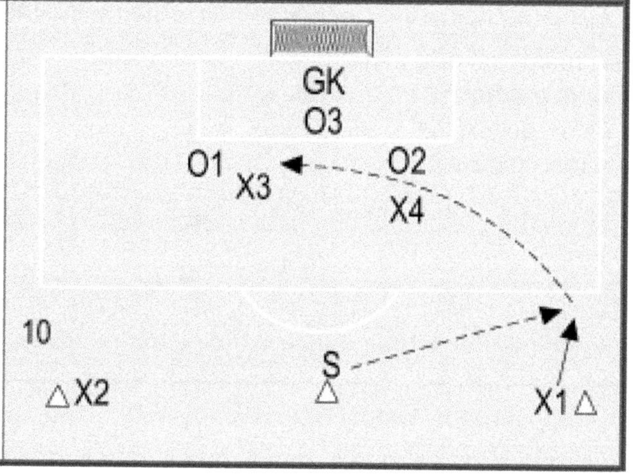

GK
O3
O1
X3
O2
X4
10
X2
S
X1

Defending As A Team

Defending as a Team

Key Factors :

TIME 30mins

1. The opposition should always be kept in front of the defence.
2. Keep both the opposing players and the ball in view.
3. Always turn into the play.
4. Deny space to the back of the defence.

Equipment : Goal and penalty area , 10 balls , cones, bibs

Practice Sequence 1:
15 minutes
The server passes the ball to X1 who then plays with X2 while the defenders O1 and O2 defend as a team.

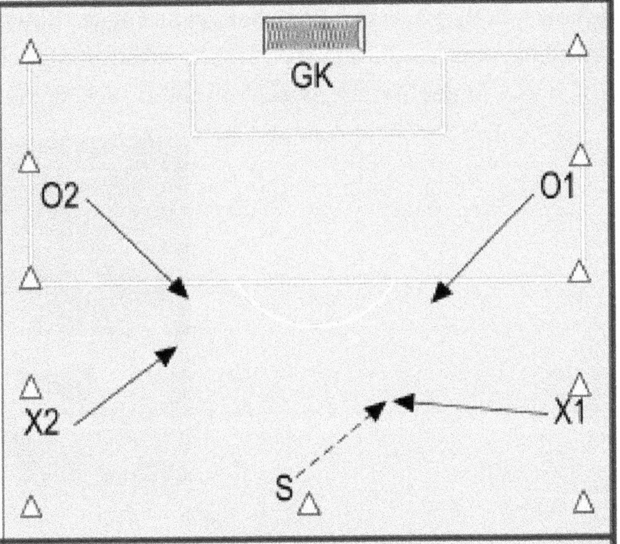

Practice Sequence 2:
15 minutes
The server passes the ball to X1 who then plays together with the other attacking players X2,X3 and X4.
The defenders O1,O2,O3 and O4 defend as a team creating a 4 v 4 situation.

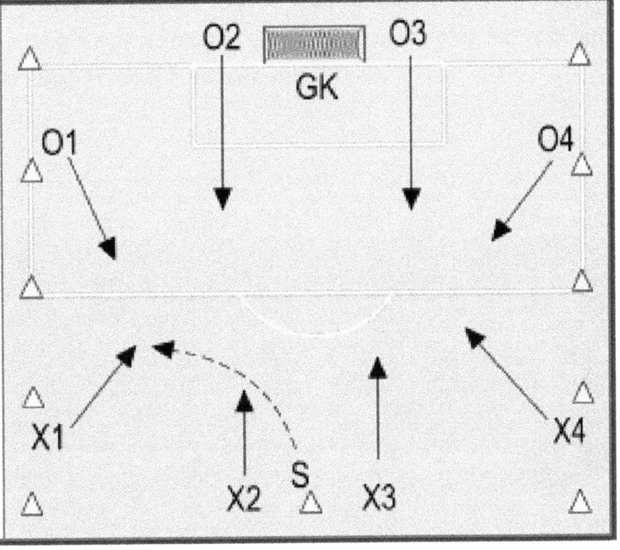

Shooting To Score

Why is soccer shooting so important? Let's just make this point right up front....the goal of soccer is to score goals! In order the score goals you need to SHOOT! Sounds basic right? Well it is amazing how quickly players and coaches get all bogged down with all the other parts of the game, defending, possession, set plays, tactics, substitutions, conditioning etc. They often forget that the game is all about sticking the ball in the back of the net!

My advice is to make sure that at least 60% of a practice is devoted to soccer shooting. This drastically improves the odds of scoring goals in games, the players enjoy it and if done right it can also be a tremendous way of conditioning players.

Basic Shooting

Basic Shooting

Key Factors

TIME 30mins:

1. Check the position of the goalkeeper.
2. Accuracy of the shot over power.
3. Head down and steady with the eyes on the ball.
4. Strike middle or top half of the ball.

Equipment : Goal and penalty area , 10 balls

Practice Sequence 1:
10 minutes
The Goalkeeper throws the ball to each player in turn and each player controls the ball and takes a shot on goal.

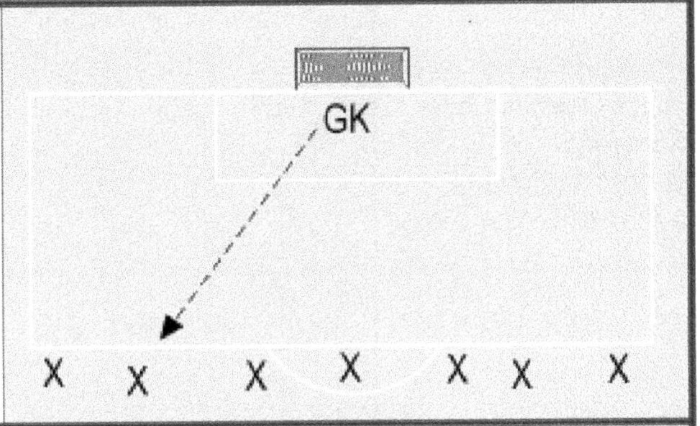

GK
X X X X X X X

Practice Sequence 2:
10 minutes
X1 passes the ball to the server who returns the pass.
The ball is played by the server in the path of the running X player who shoots for a goal without controlling the ball first.

Practice Sequence 3:
10 minutes
This is the same set up as practice 2 but this time the server throws the ball in the air in the path of the running X player who controls the ball and shoots.

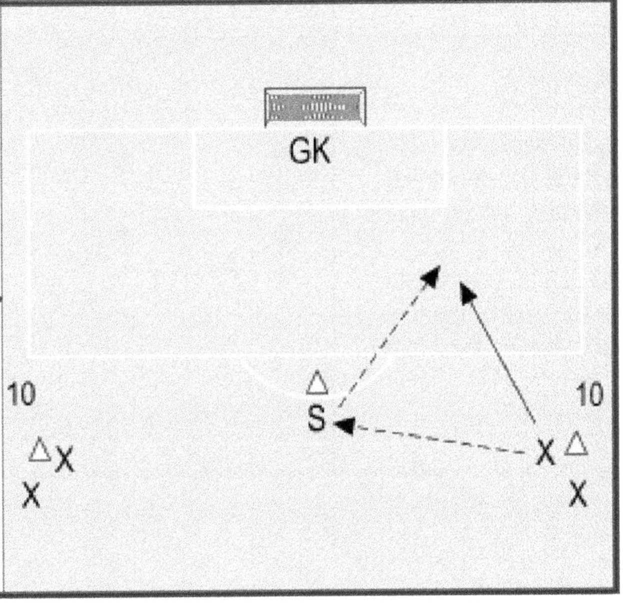

GK
10 10
S
X X
X X

Shooting across the Goal

Key Factors : TIME 30mins

1. Check the position of the goalkeeper.
2. Accuracy of the shot to the far post.
3. Head down and steady with the eyes on the ball.
4. Strike middle or top half of the ball.

Equipment : Goal and penalty area , 10 balls , cones, bibs

Practice Sequence 1:
15 minutes
The X player passes the ball to the server who returns the pass in the path of the X player.
X collects the pass and controls the ball for a shot across the goal.

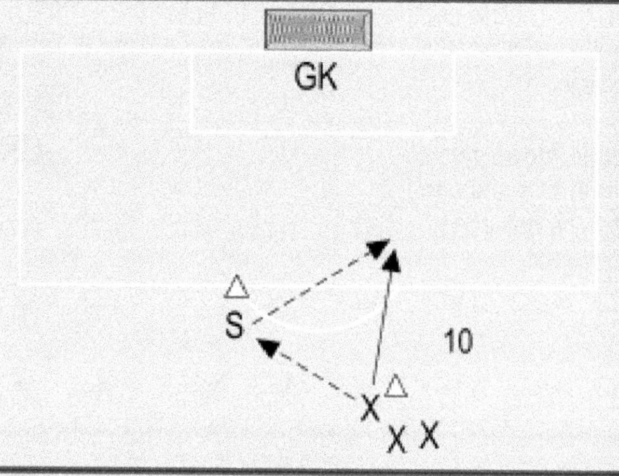

Practice Sequence 2:
15 minutes
This is the same set up as practice 1 but the O defender is included in the play to threaten the X players.
This time the X2 player runs into the funnel at the back of the goal after the ball is passed back to X1.

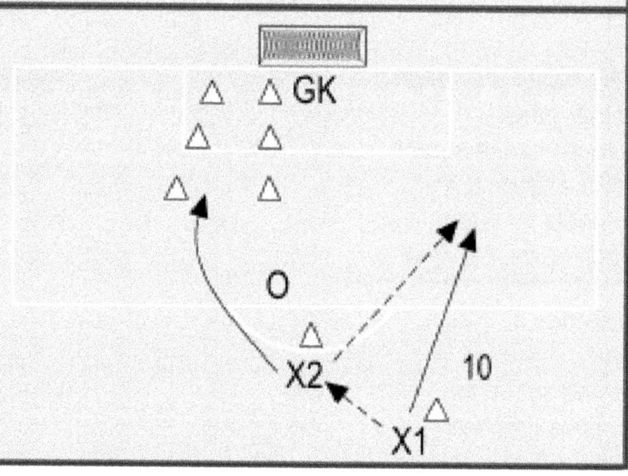

Active Shooting

Active Shooting

TIME 30mins

Key Factors :

1. Check the position of the goalkeeper.
2. Accuracy over power.
3. Shoot on first opportunity if within range and not blocked by an opponent.
4. If it is not possible to shoot, pass to a player with a better opportunity.

Equipment : 2 goals and grid 40 X 40, 10 balls, bibs , cones

Practice Sequence 1:
15 minutes
The goalkeeper throws the ball to a player in their team.
Any player can shoot from the back grid.
The 2, O or X players in the forward grid can only pass back to their players in the back grid.
All players must stay inside their half of the practice grid.

Practice Sequence 2:
15 minutes
Any X player or O player can shoot from the back grid.
The 2, O or X players in the forward grid, can continue to pass back to their players in the back grid or a one touch shot on the goal.

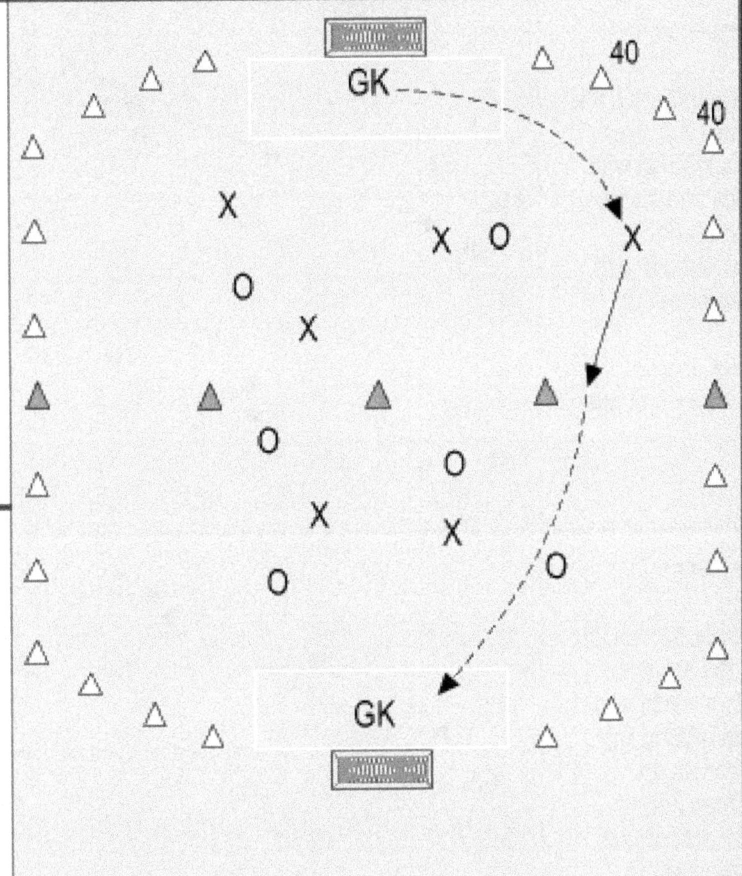

Running and Shooting

Key Factors :

TIME 30mins

1. Run at controlled speed.
2. Check the position of the goalkeeper.
3. Eyes on the ball with body over the ball and do not overreach.
4. Shoot for accuracy rather than power.

Equipment : Grids created from cones, 10 balls ,bibs

Practice Sequence 1:
15 minutes
The goalkeeper throws the ball to the next X player who controls the ball with the first touch and shoots with the next touch.
The X player should wait until the goalkeeper is ready.
The X players should retrieve their own ball after each shot.

40 30 X XXX 8 GK GK 8 X X X X

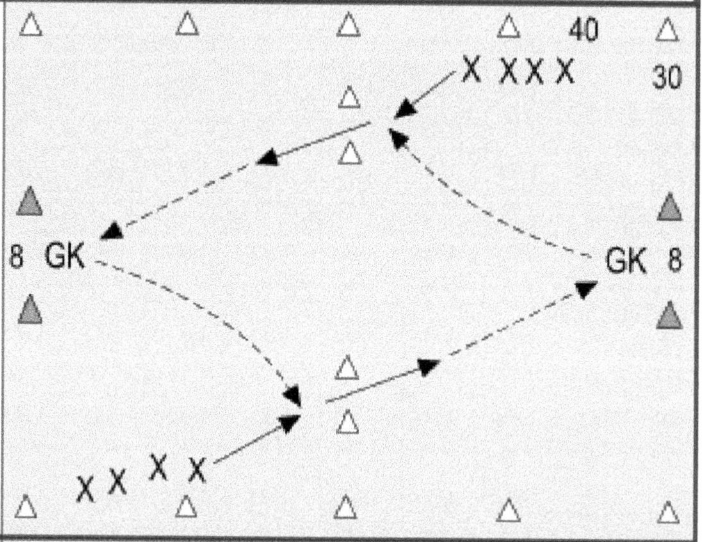

Practice Sequence 2:
15 minutes
The goalkeeper throws the ball to the next X player who controls the ball and then dribbles around the cones and shoots on exiting the three cones.
The X player should wait until the goalkeeper is ready.
The X players should retrieve their own ball after each shot.

40 30 X XXX 8 GK GK 8 X X X X

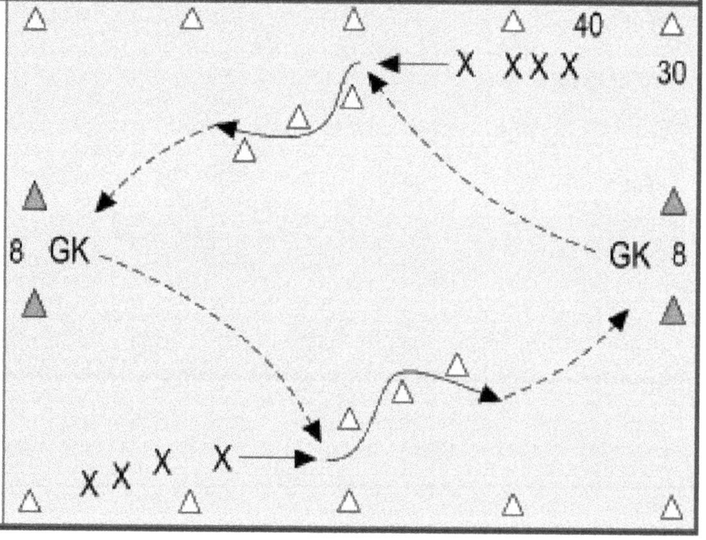

Turning and Creating Space to Shoot

TIME 30mins

Key Factors :

1. Create space from the opponent by running sideways onto the ball.
2. Receive the ball with foot furthest away from opponent.
3. Turn and receive the ball in one move and shoot at first opportunity.
4. Supporting player runs to create space to receive the ball.

Equipment : Goal and penalty area, 10 balls, bibs , cones

Practice Sequence 1:
10 minutes
The X player runs to receive the ball from one of the servers, controls the ball and shoots.
Practice with players coming from both sides of the goal.

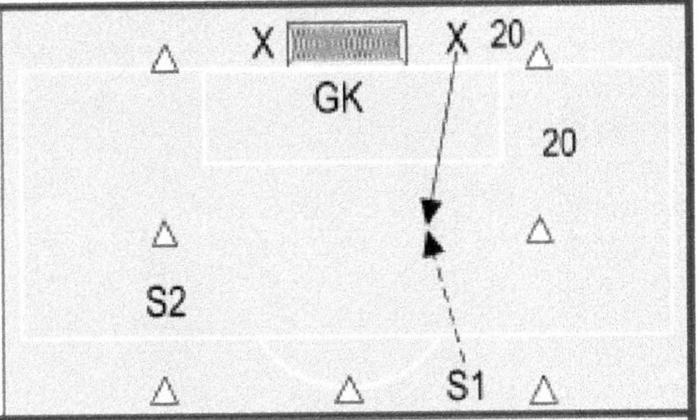

Practice Sequence 2:
10 minutes
The X player runs to receive the ball from one of the servers, controls the ball and shoots.
The O player acts a defender to prevent the X player from turning.
Practice with players coming from both sides of the goal.

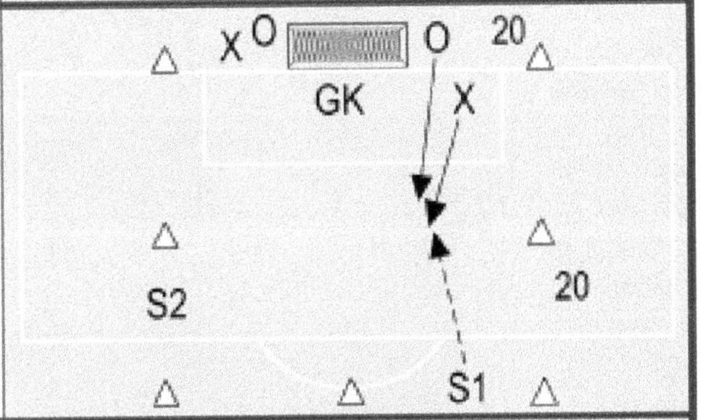

Practice Sequence 3:
10 minutes
One of the X players runs to collect the ball from one of the servers, while the other X player creates space to receive a possible pass.
Both X players play together for a shot on the goal.
The O players defend to prevent the X players from scoring.

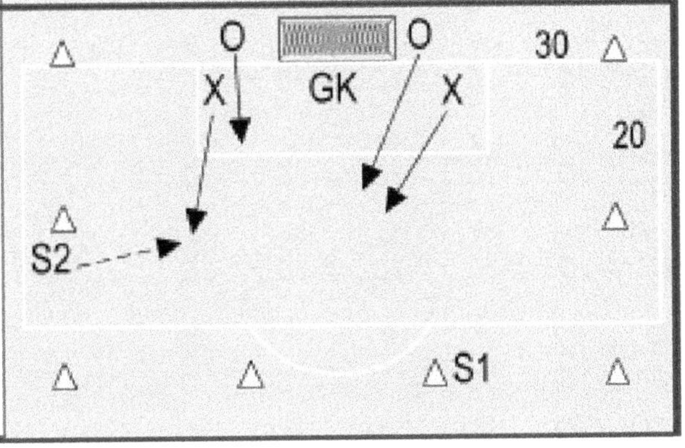

Shooting from a Distance

Key Factors :

TIME 20mins

1. Observe position and the movement of the goalkeeper.
2. Selection of shot.
3. Accuracy over power.
4. Get well up to the ball to avoid overreaching.

Equipment : Small sided field 60 X 40 yards, 10 balls, bibs, cones

Starting Position:
X6 passes the ball to O3 who passes to X5 and the play is active. Alternate the starting position to X5/O4/X6 and X6/O3/X5.

Practice Sequence :
When O3 has passed the ball to X5 the practice is live.
All other X players should make space to allow X5 to either dribble the ball or make a pass to another X player.
O1/ O2 and X5/X6 are the only players allowed in the attacking third but X5/X6 must pass back out of the attacking third to shoot.
All X players can shoot at any time but outside the attacking third.

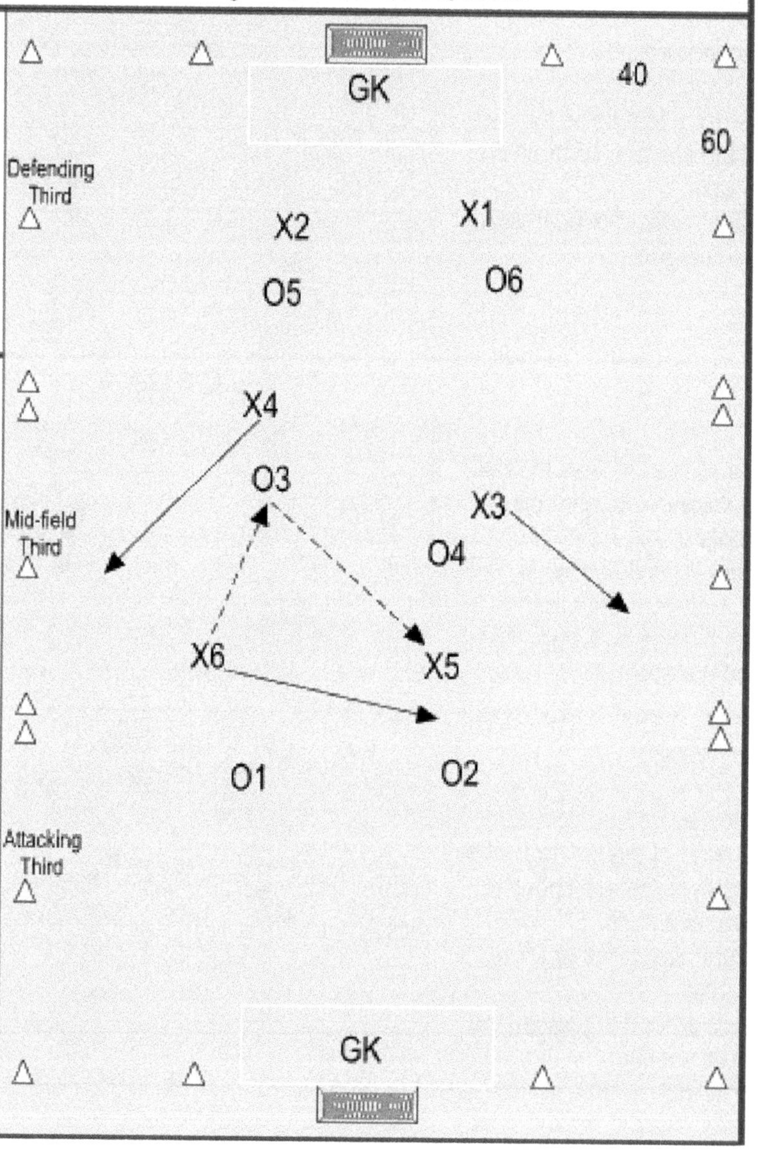

Attacking And Shooting Around The Gaol

Attacking and Shooting around the Goal

TIME 20mins

Key Factors :

1. Observe the position and the movement of the goalkeeper.
2. Shoot from inside the V grid only.
3. Pass or cross from outside the V grid.
4. Selection and accuracy of the shot..

Equipment : Small sided field 60 X 40 yards, 10 balls, bibs, cones

Starting Position :
X3 starts with the ball and make a pass to O4 and O4 then passes to X4.
Switch the start point between X3/O4/X4 and X4/O3/X3.

Practice Sequence :
When O4 has passed the ball to to X4 the practice is live.
Both X5 and X6 must create enough space to receive the ball.
Only O1 and O2 are allowed inside the attacking third, but the four X players X3, X4, X5 and X6 are allowed inside the attacking third.

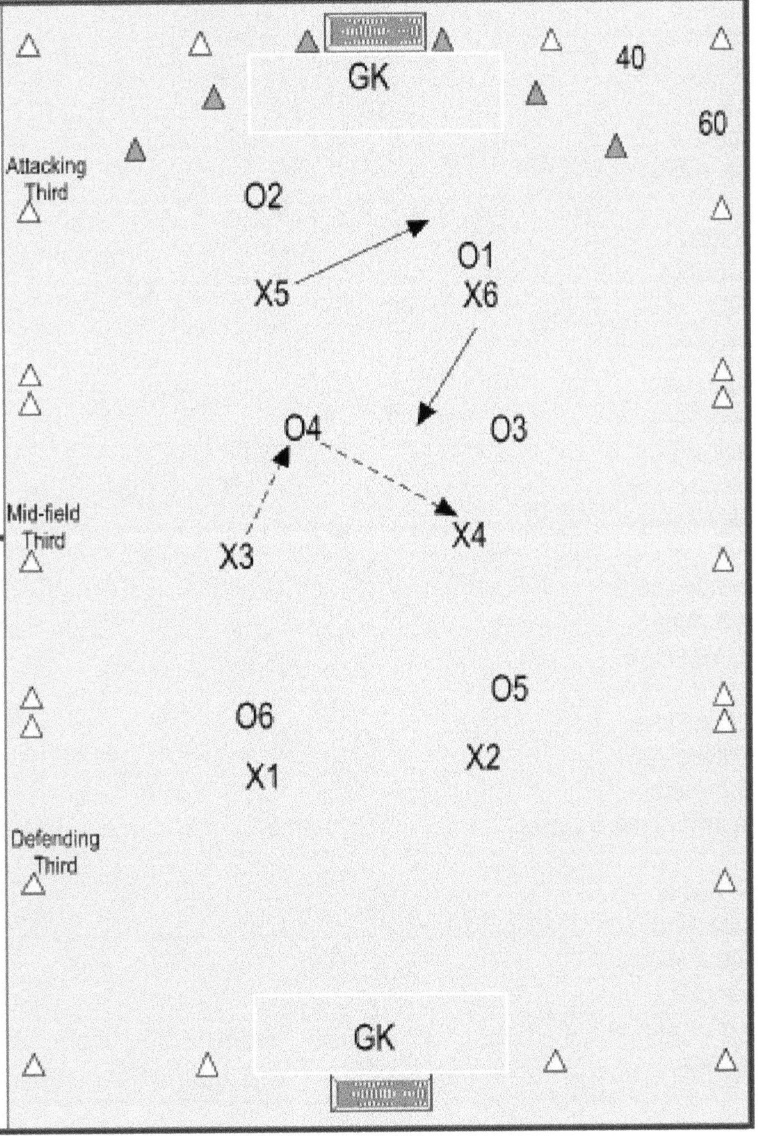

Creating Shooting Opportunities

Key Factors :

TIME 20mins

1. Check the position of the defence and the goalkeeper.
2. Accuracy over power.
3. Shoot on first opportunity if within range and not blocked by an opponent.
4. If it is not possible to shoot, pass to a player with a better opportunity.

Equipment : Small sided field 60 X 40 created with cones, divided into thirds, 10 balls, bibs

Starting Position :
X3 passes to O3 who passes to X4.
X4 should make a forward pass to X6, X5 or X3.
Alternate starting between X3/O3/X4 and X4/O4/X3.

Practice Sequence :
Coach the X players.
X5 and X6 should create space from their respective defending players.
X3 should create space.
The O players must stay in their respective thirds.
While the X team is in possession of the ball one of the X players can join that third of the field.
For example X3 can play in the attacking third while the X team is in possession of the ball, but O4 must stay in the mid-field third.

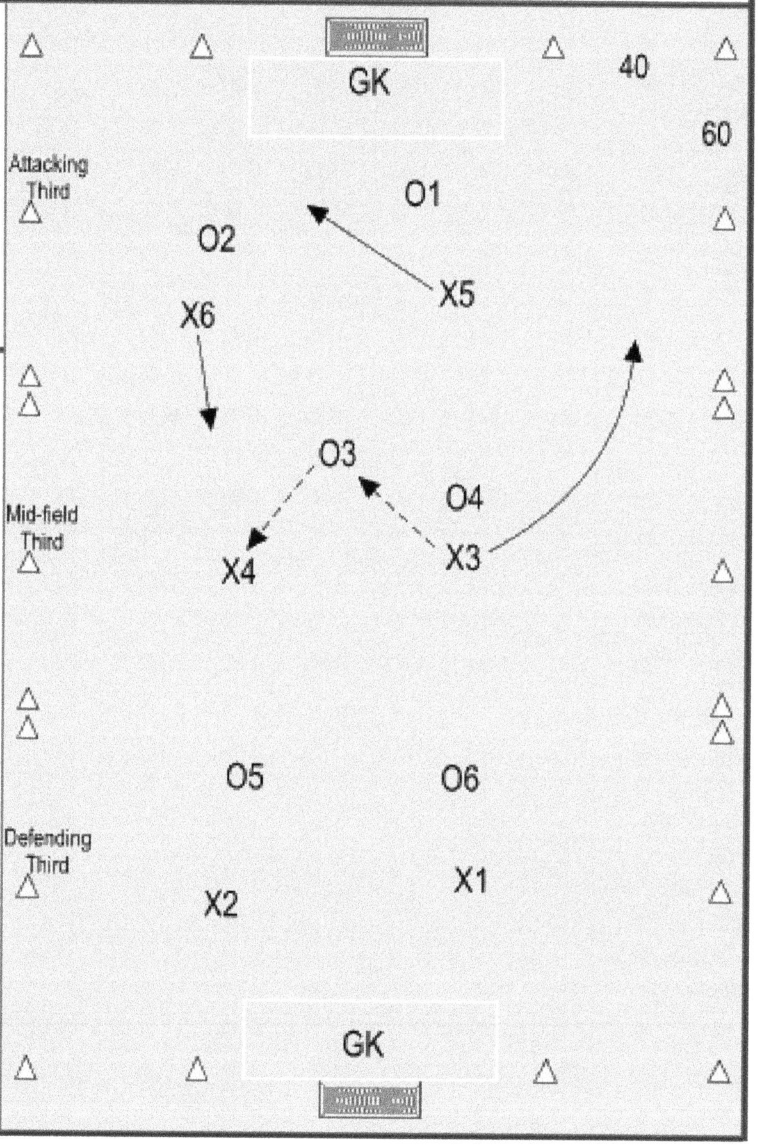

When And When Not To Shoot

When and When not to Shoot

TIME 30mins

Key Factors :

1. Shoot inside the shooting area.
2. Shoot within the range of the players' ability.
3. Do not shoot if an opponent can block the shot.
4. Dribble or pass the ball from outside the shooting area.

Equipment : Goal and penalty area , 10 balls , cones, bibs

Practice Sequence 1:
15 minutes
X1 passes to the server who passes the ball to X2 .
X2 should shoot if possible inside the shooting area otherwise dribble or pass into the area for a shot.
The defender O can threaten X2 as soon as the server passes the ball .

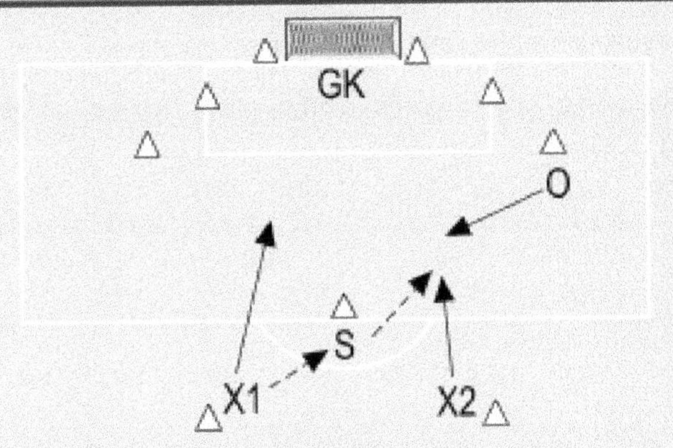

Practice Sequence 2:
15 minutes
X1 passes to the server.
The server passes to either X2 or X3 who should shoot if possible otherwise pass to one of the other attackers.
The two defenders O1 and O2 can threaten the attacking players as soon as the ball is passed from X1.

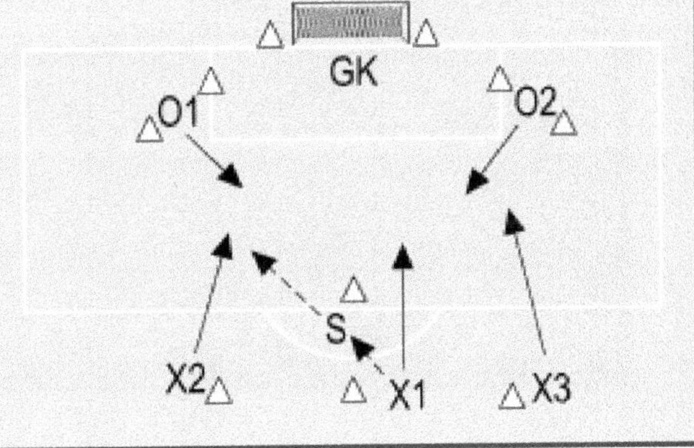

Crossing The Ball

Crossing in soccer has a strong negative impact on scoring: Stronger teams have more options how to score and open play

crossing seems as one of the suboptimal ways of a goal creation.

Teams such as Arsenal, Chelsea, Liverpool, Manchester City or Tottenham have a potential of scoring an extra goal per match if they reduced open crossing. A reversed picture is seen in the defense.

analysis, more goal opportunities are missed in general when crossing against weak teams than crossing against strong teams. Interestingly.

the actual conversion of open crosses to goals plays only a minor role for explaining the impact of open crossing on goals.

Running And Crossing The Ball

Running and Crossing the ball

TIME 30mins:

Key Factors

1. Run at controlled speed.
2. Eyes should be on the ball each time the ball is being kicked.
3. Keep head up while running.
4. Cross the ball with a lofted pass into the target area.

Equipment : Goal and penalty area , 10 balls , cones, bibs

Practice Sequence 1:
10 minutes
X runs with the ball until middle of the last 10 X 10 grid and passes to the next player.
The next X player repeats the process in the opposite direction.

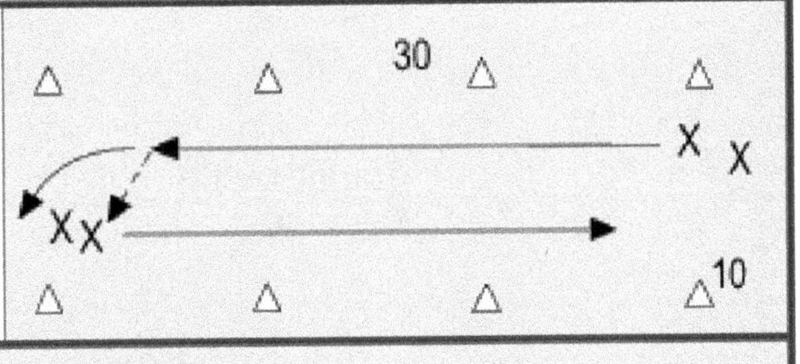

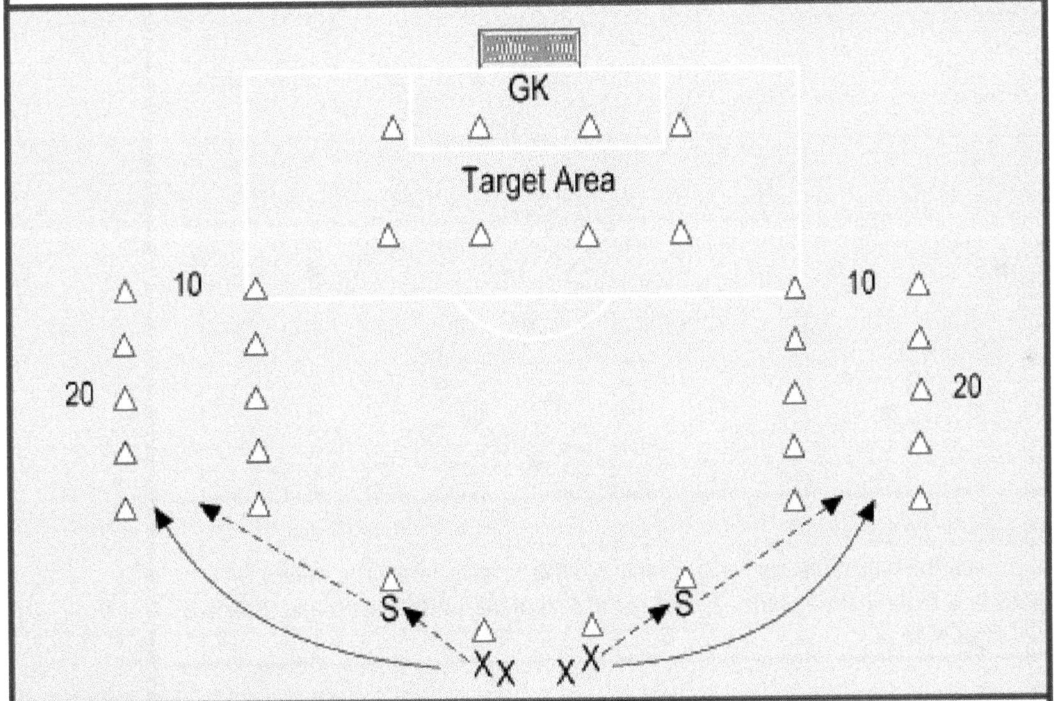

Practice Sequence 2: 20 minutes
The X players take turns to pass the ball to sever and run into the crossing lane and collect the returned pass. The X player then runs to the end of the crossing lane and makes a cross into the target area.

Attacking by Crossing the Ball

Key Factors : TIME 30mins

1. The crosses should be played early into the target area.
2. The attacker nearest the ball should make a run for the near post.
3. The attacker furthest from the ball should make a run for the far post.
4. Attackers should keep behind the player crossing the ball.

Equipment : Goal and penalty area, running lanes, 10 balls, bibs

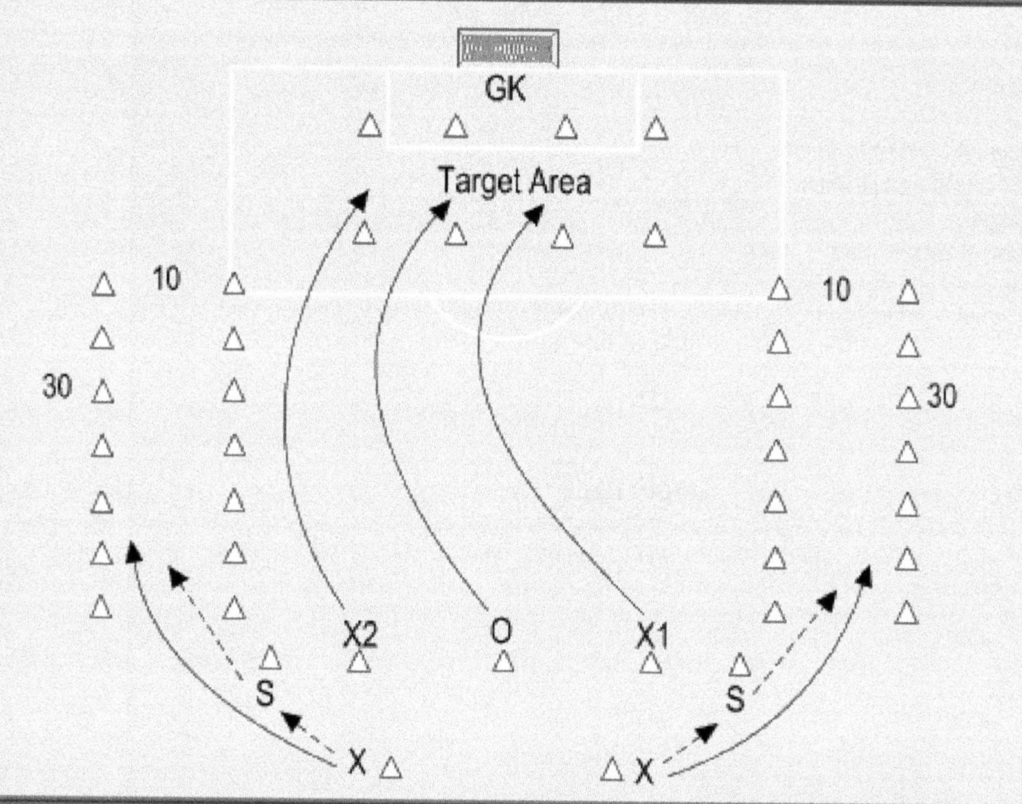

Practice Sequence 1: 10 minutes
The X player passes the ball to the server and runs into the running lane. The server S returns the pass to X in the running lane. X runs to the end of the running lane and makes a cross into the target area.

Practice Sequence 2: 10 minutes
The X1 player starts and makes an angled run to the near post, collecting the cross, keeping on side behind the player crossing the ball.

Practice Sequence 3: 10 minutes
The X2 player is added to the practice to make an angled run to the far post. The O player is also added as a defender.

Crossing from the End Line

Key Factors : TIME 30mins

1. Run at controlled speed to the end line keeping the ball under control.
2. Cross the ball into the target area using a ground, chip or lofted pass.
3. Attacking players should make angled runs into target area.
4. Attacking players should arrive in the penalty area facing the ball

Equipment : Goal and penalty area , 10 balls , cones, bibs

Practice Sequence 1:
15 minutes
X1 passes the ball to the sever who passes the ball back to X1.
X1 makes a controlled run with the ball to the end line and crosses the ball into the target area.
X2 runs an angled run into the target area.

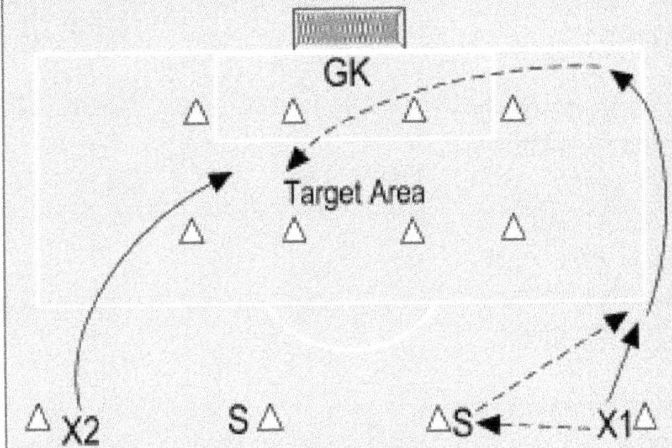

Practice Sequence 2:
15 minutes
X1 passes the ball to the server who passes the ball to X2.
X2 then passes the ball to X1 who makes an overlap run to end line to make a cross into the target area.
X2 and X3 make angled runs into the target area.
Both O1 and O2 should defend realistically.

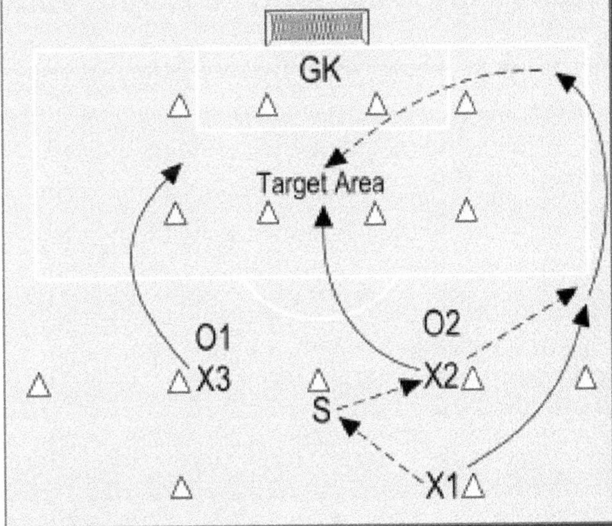

Crossing from the Side of the Penalty Area

Key Factors :

TIME 30mins

1. Run with the ball at controlled speed.
2. A lofted pass or ground pass to the opposite side of the goal area.
3. Accuracy and timing of the cross.
4. Attacking players should make an angled run into the penalty.

Equipment : Goal and penalty area , 10 balls , cones, bibs

Practice Sequence 1:
15 minutes
X plays the ball to the server who returns the pass into the path of the X player.
X collects the pass and controls the ball for a cross into the target area on the opposite side of the goal area.
The cross is delivered outside the penalty area.
Practice with both right and left crosses.

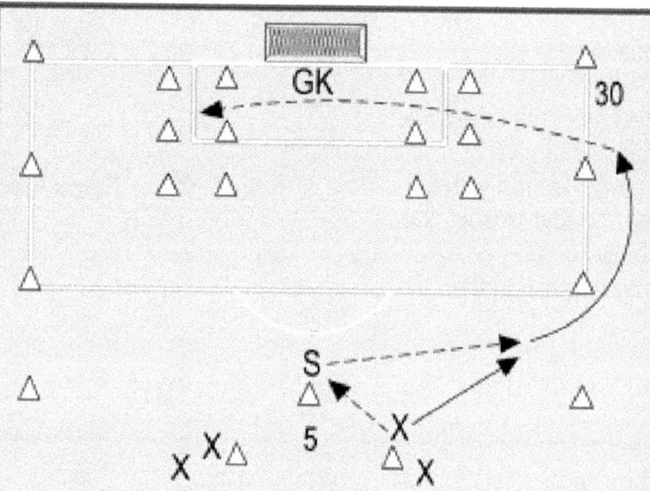

Practice Sequence 2:
15 minutes
X1 plays the ball to X3 who returns the pass into the path of X1.
X1 collects the pass and controls the ball and runs outside the penalty area for a cross into the target zone on the opposite side of the goal area.
X2 and X3 make angled runs into the target area.
O1 and O2 defend against X1 and X2.
Practice with both right and left crosses.

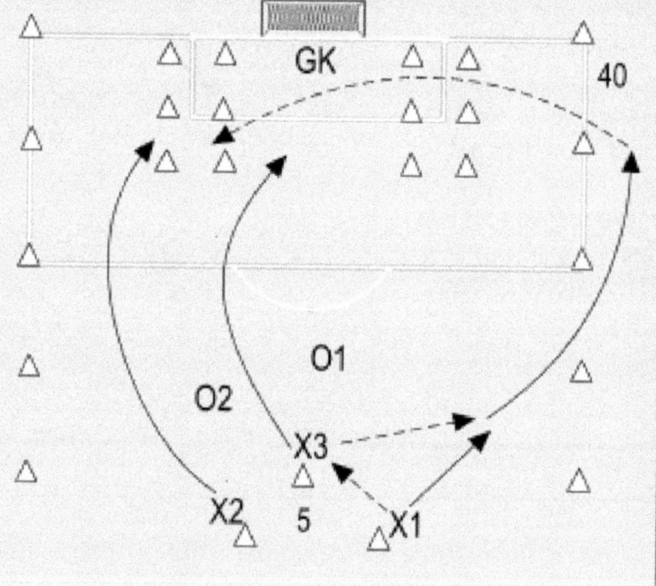

Attacking in Front of the Goal

Key Factors TIME 30mins:

1. Create space to receive the ball.
2. Attack the ball with the head or foot.
3. The timing of the run or movement to the ball.
4. Get in front of the defender and be first to the ball.

Equipment : Goal and penalty area , grids created from cones, 10 balls, bibs

Practice Sequence 1: 10 minutes The server makes a lofted pass to the X player who attacks the ball to score a goal. The O players defend to prevent the X players from scoring.	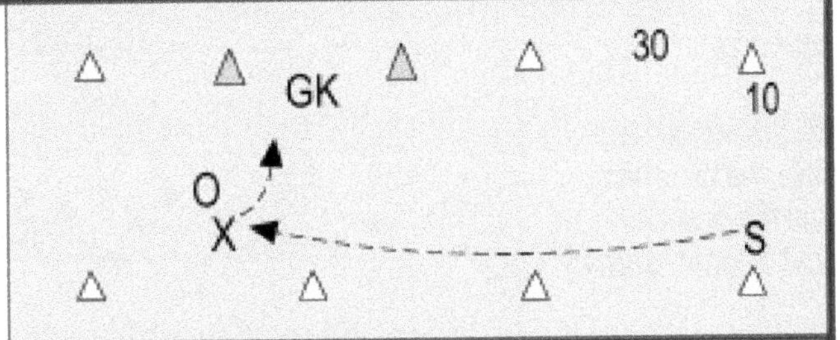
Practice Sequence 2: 10 minutes The server makes a lofted pass to the X players who attack the ball to score a goal. The O players defend to prevent the X players from scoring.	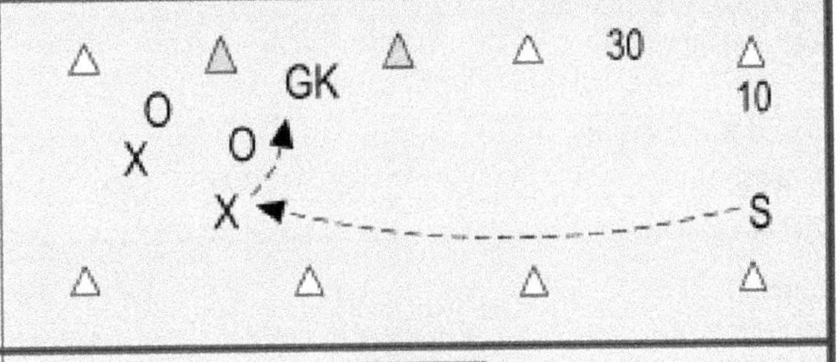
Practice Sequence 3: 10 minutes The center server passes to one of the servers at the side of the penalty area, who then makes a ground or lofted pass into the penalty area. The X players inside the penalty area should attempt to score while the O players defend the area.	

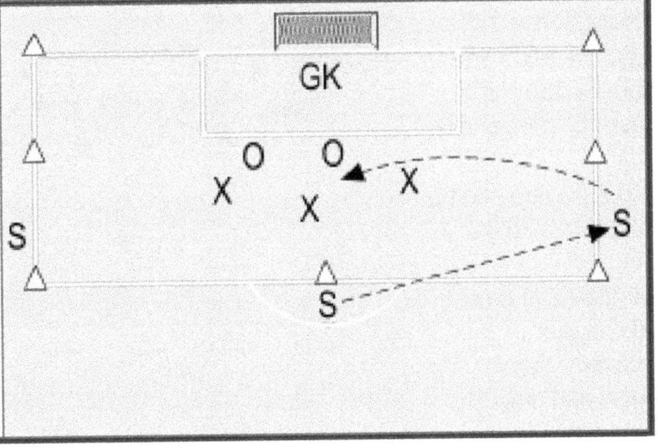

Finishing from Crosses

Key Factors : TIME 30mins

1. Create space by moving in the opposite direction to the crossing player.
2. Attack when the crossing player's head goes down to cross the ball.
3. Move in front of opponents as the cross comes in.
4. Be first and attack the ball.

Equipment : Goal and penalty area , 10 balls , cones, bibs

Practice Sequence 1:
15 minutes
X1 passes to the server and runs to receive the returned pass, controls the ball and makes a cross into the penalty area.
The attacking X players attempt to make a first time shot on goal.
Use both X1 and X2 to create left and right crosses.

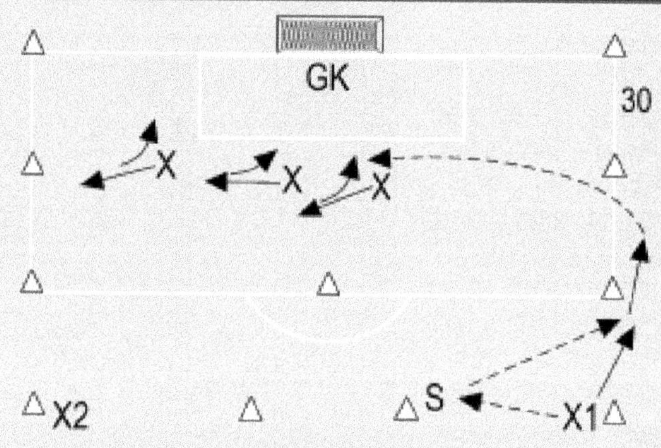

Practice Sequence 2:
15 minutes
X1 passes to the server and runs to receive the returned pass, controls the ball and makes a cross into the penalty area.
The attacking X players attempt to make a first time shot on goal.
Use both X1 and X2 to create left and right crosses.
The 2 O defenders should protect the goal and defend realistically.

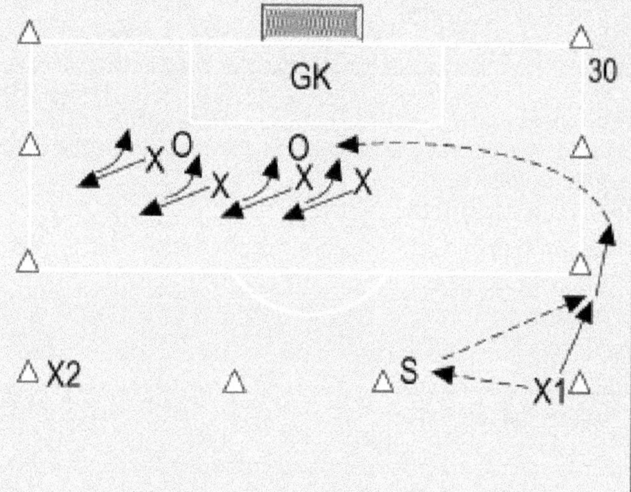

Attacking with Crosses

Key Factors : TIME 20mins

1. Cross the ball early behind the defence.
2. Attackers should observe the position of the defence and the goalkeeper.
3. The attacker's angle and timing of the run.
4. Attackers should be first to the ball.

Equipment : Small sided field 60 X 40 yards, 10 yard running lanes, 10 balls, bibs, cones

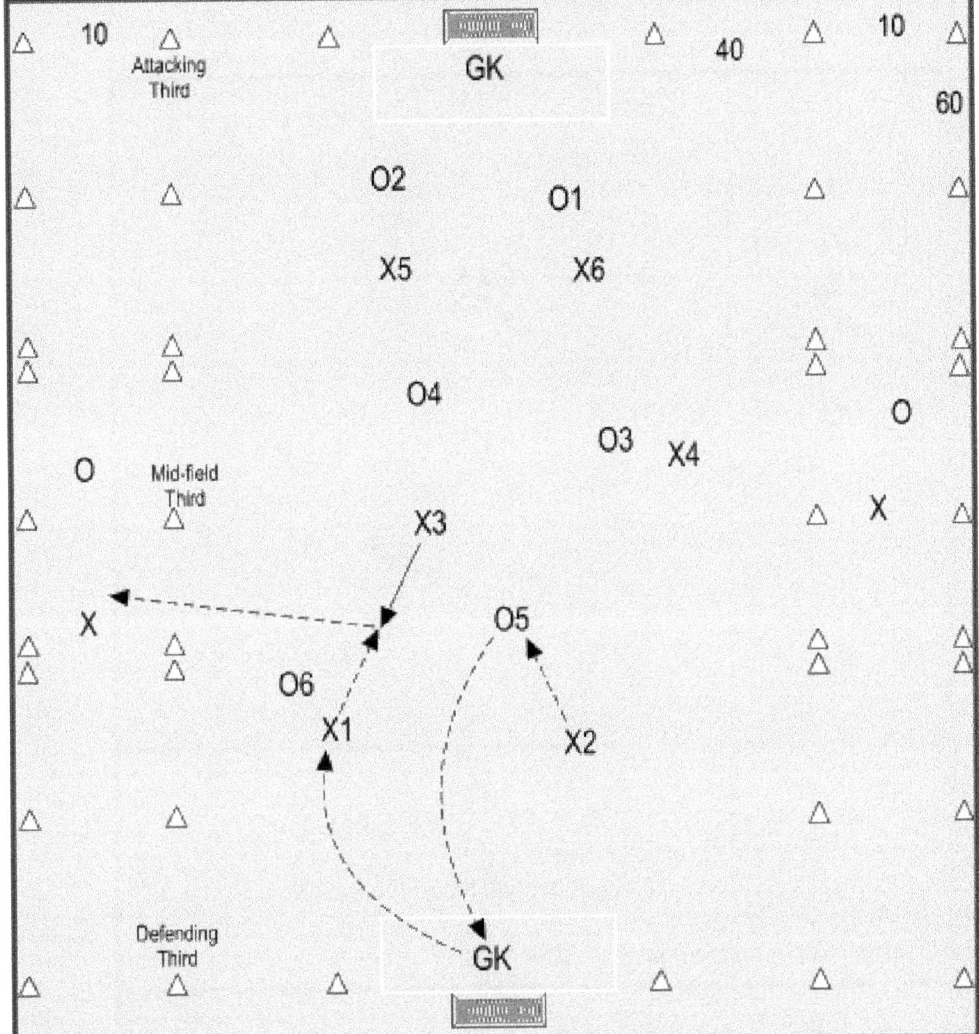

Starting Position :
X2 starts with the ball and makes a pass to O5 and O5 then kicks the ball back to the goalkeeper. The goalkeeper throws the ball to X1 who passes to the oncoming X3 and X3 should make a pass to the crossing player in the crossing lane.
Switch the start point between X2/O5 /X1 and X1/O6/X2.

Practice Sequence :
When O5 has kicked the ball back to the goalkeeper the practice is live.
The X players must use the crossing players and the X players cannot score a goal unless the ball has first been played to a crossing player in the same practice sequence.
Only the crossing players are allowed inside the crossing lanes.

Crossing and finishing

Key Factors : TIME 20mins

1. Run at controlled speed with the ball under control.
2. Cross the ball using a ground, chip or lofted pass.
3. Create space away from the opponent by moving the opposite direction to the ball.
4. Time to move is when the crossing players head goes down to cross the ball.

Equipment : Half a soccer field with the goal and penalty area, 10 balls, bibs, cones

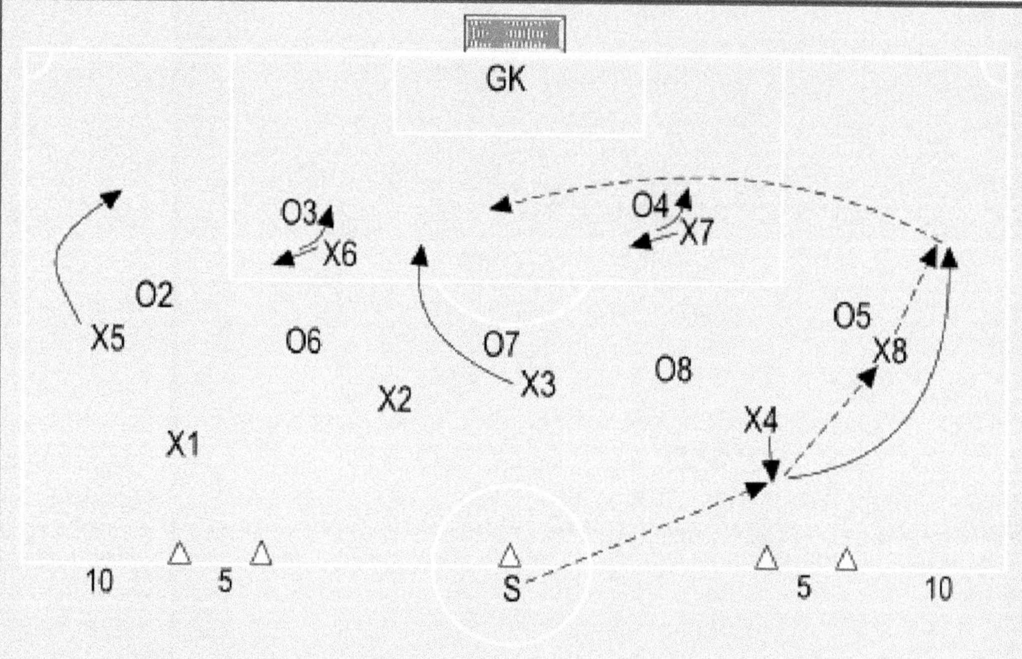

Starting Position :
Move all players out of the penalty area.
The server plays the ball to X4 and the practice is live.
X4 controls the ball and passes to X8 and makes an overlap run to receive the return pass, and crosses the ball into the penalty area.
Alternate the start between X4/X8 on the right to X1/X5 on the left.

Practice Sequence: Coach the X players.
The midfield player X4 runs to collect the ball from the server and passes to the outside mid-field player X8 and makes an overlap run. The return pass should be in the path of X4 and then X4 should make a cross into the penalty area.
The attackers should be prepared to receive the ball and make a good attempt to score.
The central mid-field players should also be prepared to make an angled run into the area to score when possible.
The O defending players should defend against the X players realistically.

BOOK END

www.ingramcontent.com/pod-product-compliance
Ingram Content Group UK Ltd.
Pitfield, Milton Keynes, MK11 3LW, UK
UKHW051136260726
13967UKWH00010B/3084

9 781365 917837